A Study of 2 Timothy

BETH MOORE

with articles by
MELISSA MOORE

LifeWay Press®
Nashville, Tennessee

Published by LifeWay Press®. © 2016 Beth Moore

ISBN 978-1-4300-5500-6 • Item 006103964

Dewey Decimal Classification: 248.84
Subject Headings: FAITH \ DISCIPLESHIP \ WITNESSING

Cover design and photography: Micah Kandros

Illustrations: Kristi Smith, Juicebox Designs

To order additional copies of this resource, write to LifeWay Church Resources Customer Service; One LifeWay Plaza; Nashville, TN 37234-0113; fax 615.251.5933; phone toll free 800.458.2772; email *customerservice@lifeway.com*; order online at *www.lifeway.com*; or visit the LifeWay Christian Store serving you.

Printed in the United States of America

Adult Ministry Publishing, LifeWay Church Resources, One LifeWay Plaza, Nashville, TN 37234-0152

Dedication

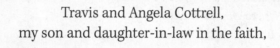

Travis and Angela Cottrell,
my son and daughter-in-law in the faith,

I knew from the start that, if Jesus graced me
to see this series to a finish, I would dedicate it to you.
You are second in my heart to my own children
and there you will stay,
come rain or shine, until I see Christ's beautiful face.

I don't think the apostle would mind if, on this occasion,
I borrowed the fitting words he used to describe his beloved Timothy.

"For I have no one like him."
Philippians 2:20, ESV

Contents

WEEK FOUR
DIFFICULT TIMES, DIFFICULT PEOPLE

WEEK FIVE
FULFILL YOUR MINISTRY

SESSION SIX VIDEO
FACE TO FACE

About the Authors

Beth Moore is a best-selling book and Bible study author and a dynamic teacher whose conferences take her across the globe. Beth lives in Houston, Texas, where she leads Living Proof Ministries with the purpose of encouraging and teaching women to know and love Jesus through the study of Scripture.

Beth and her husband, Keith, have two adult daughters and three delightful grandchildren. They are devoted to the local church and have the privilege of attending Bayou City Fellowship in Houston, Texas.

Her life is full of activity, but one commitment remains constant: counting all things but loss for the excellence of knowing Christ Jesus, the Lord (Phil. 3:8).

Melissa Moore has served as research and writing assistant to Beth Moore since earning her M.A. in Biblical Exegesis from Wheaton College in 2007. She has since received her Th.M. in New Testament from Columbia Theological Seminary. She currently resides in Houston, Texas, with a poorly behaved and not-so-suitable companion named Shadowfax the Weimaraner. When she is not working on a teaching or writing project with her mom, she enjoys working part-time on a M.A. in Biblical Languages at Houston Baptist University. She loves the arts, the outdoors, and all things related to Bible and theology.

entrusted

About this Study

entrusted is designed for both interactive personal study and group discussion. Here are a few suggestions for making your time with the study more meaningful.

To enhance your learning and application of Scripture, the study is written in an interactive format. I encourage you to complete all of the written work in your workbook. This isn't just fill-in-the-blanks. The interactive questions represent the very places where we'd look together in Scripture as we shared a cup of French roast coffee together. Please don't let the word "homework" scare you. The Holy Spirit uses your efforts as you respond to the activities in your own words.

I so wish I could be personally present with you each week in your personal study time and in your group time. This interactive format provides the most personal contact possible until the time we can share that cup of coffee. Then I'll look forward to listening to you as you have graciously listened to me through all these studies. I pray that you will gain as much from this journey as I have. Thank you for the privilege to serve you.

This may be our first series together, and, if so, I pray with all of my heart that this in-depth study and others like it will fan a lifelong flame in your heart for God's Word. Perhaps we've studied together before and, if so, I'm thrilled to tell you that this one earned its own place in my heart. Each series from *A Woman's Heart: God's Dwelling Place* to this one has been used by God to accomplish a distinctive and lasting work in me. The mention of each name stirs up the remembrance of that prevailing revelation.

I won't tell you in advance what God worked in my life through this journey, because the fun of it for me is to process the material along the way with you. When I pen Week One, Day One of any study, I have no clearer idea where we are headed than you do right now. When you get to difficult material, you will see that I am struggling through it, too. When you're convicted, you can be pretty certain I'm squirming, too. I love the uncertainty of what's ahead as long as I'm in the security of God's hands. It's like driving a winding highway in a convertible for the very first time. I want to feel the wind in my face. If you do too, we're going to make good traveling partners.

As we have in the last two Bible studies, we are offering you options. Goodness knows we need a few of those amid frantic schedules and demanding roles.

You get to choose your own level of participation.

Level 1: *Participate in the video sessions only*

Through the years I've watched people drop out of weekly Bible study because they couldn't keep up with the homework. Don't think for a moment that if you can't do all of it, you're better off doing none of it. A shorter time in Scripture is far better than none at all. Watch the video sessions even if you can't get your homework assignments accomplished.

LEVEL 2: Participate in the video sessions
> *+ do the weekly homework assignments*

Moving up to level 2 in which you meet with God on the pages of Scripture numerous times each week exponentially increases your experience. When you turn the last page, you will truly know 2 Timothy and the important circumstances surrounding Paul's final letter. If you've got the stamina to do the homework (and you do!), you've got it in you to view the sessions. Keep in mind that many of the larger themes are addressed in the sessions, so try your hardest to view the coinciding ones at the end of each week of homework.

LEVEL 3: Participate in the video sessions
> + do the weekly homework assignments
> *+ handwrite 2 Timothy*

I'm really excited about this level! For the third time in more than 20 years of writing Bible studies, we've arrived at a book of the Bible short enough to invite this exercise. During Session One of this series, and in the homework that follows we'll set the context for the letter. Session Six video will wrap everything up with a final challenge. But in sessions Two through Five, and the corresponding weeks of homework, we'll dig into the actual letter of 2 Timothy. Each time we come to a new segment of the letter, I will ask you to read it and then handwrite it in the back of your Bible study book on the pages designed for this exercise. If you don't choose level 3, you'll simply read the portion—without a hint of self-condemnation, I pray. This option is simply available for those who want to take the next step to retain what they're learning.

LEVEL 4: Participate in the video sessions
> + do the weekly homework assignments
> + handwrite 2 Timothy
> *+ read "Next Level with Melissa"*

You might say I'm particularly partial to this level since I'm her mother. I say that with a grin but, while that's true, the real reason we incorporated this level is because you—or people like you—asked for it. Many have written me after a series and asked how they could go even deeper in the material. We first responded to their request with Melissa's articles in *James: Mercy Triumphs*. She's back this time by popular demand.

Woodrow Wilson once said, "I not only use all the brains I have but all I can borrow."[1] Good advice, if you ask me; so once again, I've borrowed my daughter Melissa's brain. And it's a big one. She has far surpassed her mother in formal theological training and the use of original languages, so I've asked her to bring a more academic approach to several of our concepts each week. Please keep in mind that her portions are options and that, stylistically, they are exactly what I asked of her.

Melissa and I know up front that neither of our writings will suit everyone's tastes, but we partner with a deep and sincere desire to serve you more fully. I would gladly have added her name to the cover, but she asked that I refrain. In years past, my daughter Amanda was very involved in the Bible study process as my first reader and editor. These days she has her hands full as mom to my beloved grandchildren and as pastor's wife to a rapidly growing church in Houston. You can know that she joins Melissa and me in serving you through this series as your number one intercessor. We wrote and she prayed.

Trying to picture some of your faces almost has me tickled. But don't blame me. Remember all those who kept asking for more? Blame them. Beloved, if you commit to all five of these levels, 2 Timothy will live in the marrow of your bones—probably for the rest of your life. You'll find a short tutorial on the *Entrusted* website (*lifeway.com/entrusted*) and in the DVD bonus material that may help you if you're interested in this level.

Needless to say, we're not recommending trying to memorize all of 2 Timothy in the five short weeks of this series. The best recommendation for setting your pace is whatever works.

Because God led me to take this challenge, in the process of writing this study I've recited the four chapters of 2 Timothy aloud more times than I can count. I'm not the only one who recited it as the study was underway. I was beside myself with delight when Mike Wakefield, my editor on this project, told me he was memorizing it, too. We have each loved Paul's final letter all the more because God embedded it in our hearts. Not one second you spend on Scripture memory is ever wasted. Think about doing it! Pray about it! Then, some of you, do it!

Okay, friend, which level seems the most doable for you right now?

1   **2**   **3**   **4**   **5**

I'm asking you up front because I'd like to challenge you to go one level above what seems reasonably attainable. If you're willing, stretch yourself one more level! If you're pretty sure you can reach level 1, try stretching yourself into level 2 and see what happens. All you overachievers, keep in mind that higher levels and harder work won't make God love you any more than He already does. Nor will memorizing the letter make us superior to someone else who can barely manage a few sessions. We are secure in Christ and acceptable to God through Him.

We have nothing to lose here but much Scripture to gain if we're game for a challenge. Do only what blesses and not what burdens.

I wish I had a way to express the depth of my gratitude for the privilege to walk with you through a study of Scripture. I was on a walk recently in the woods near our home and a wave of emotion overtook me as I absorbed the reality of another study coming to fruition. I said aloud to Jesus, "How could You be so kind to me? How could You have such grace? Why have You done this?" I will never be able to wrap my mind around His kind of love. His depth of mercy. Jesus pulled me out of tremendous bondage and despair. I come to you with no worthiness of my own but this I promise you, my friend: together we will pursue the One who is worthy of all the glory, honor, and praise the two of us can offer. Let's not wait another moment.

Introduction

Dear Fellow Traveler,

On a flight to Miami several months ago, I pulled two slender folders out of my briefcase containing a cross section of letters I'd received in previous weeks. Several of my team members oversee our ministry correspondence, but they keep me in the loop so I don't disconnect from the very people I yearn to serve. Detachment would stick my calling in a coffin and nail it shut. Like most people, I flourish in lively relationships and community, but spending copious hours alone is an occupational hazard all full-time writers have to accept. A simple letter can be like a long arm reaching into the vortex to pull a lonesome sanguine like me back to the sidewalk.

In this case, the sidewalk was flying through the air in a silver cylinder at an altitude of 30,000 feet. Soon I was swept into each sender's story, awed by the ways Jesus customized His signature across the snippets of their autobiographies. As I made my way to the bottom of the stack, I had a "wait a minute" moment. The thought occurred to me how many letters referenced specific ages.

I fanned them out on my tray table from the oldest to youngest and nearly wept.

Elsie was 82. She'd been involved in children's ministry at her church for 69 years. Try to wrap your mind around that kind of faithfulness. She let me know how much she loved studying the Bible and that she still had lots to learn. I knew the feeling. Angelee was turning 40. Jesus had taken her by surprise in the sacred pages and she'd fallen head over heels in love with Him. Courtney was 32. She'd given her heart to Jesus in the 8th grade and made a commitment to serve Him and to show His love to her own flesh and blood. She'd kept her commitment even at the tender age of 14 when her mother passed away. She let me know she'd soon finish up her doctoral work in the field of Biblical interpretation.

Wednesday was 21. She'd been a believer for a while but had never experienced anything particularly traumatic until two weeks earlier when her little brother was struck and killed by a car. God was carrying her through. She wanted me to know. Olivia was 15. She'd just been awarded first runner-up in a beauty pageant she'd endured with grace and integrity by keeping her darling head in the Book of Esther. Sarah was 13. She'd been in daily turmoil with all sorts of doubts and had bought herself the book, *Believing God*. The testimony in her young curly cursive of how God awakened her faith almost unraveled me.

Other writers didn't specify age but the descriptions of their seasons of life filled in the age gaps. Josh had been a pastor for 16 years. In the previous year his wife had forgiven him for a heartbreaking betrayal. Their lives were being sewn back together one stitch at a time. Chris had watched God bring his young bride back to the land of the living after a season of severe depression.

Their backdrops, settings, struggles, circumstances, and writing styles differed dramatically, but each letter, without exception, shared three gorgeously glaring denominators: *Jesus. Scripture. Transformation.*

The blood flows hot in my veins with an ever-intensifying belief in the epic fusion of those three. This is my passion. This is why I've continued to hang on tight to my desk and attempt to write Bible studies while life bucks like a bronco. This is why I have guts enough to say to anyone who will listen, *No matter who you are, where you've been, or what list of demands vies for your time, do whatever you have to do to get with Jesus and study the Scriptures.*

Because the words of Christ are spirit and life.

Because God sends forth His Word with accomplishing power.

Because the Holy Spirit can bring the Scriptures to life in any life.

Because those who let Scripture sink into their bones are transformed.

Because nothing renews our minds like the Spirit of Christ working through the Word of God.

Because God could say your name before He said, "Let there be light."

Because He's got a plan for you that you don't want to miss.

Because you matter on this planet.

And because right now, in this very season, He wanted you and me in this very Bible study. Welcome, my friend. Because Jesus is mighty, miraculous, and merciful, neither one of us will be the same when we turn the last page.

Beth Moore

Group Session One

[handwritten, top right] have you ever thought of yourself as a mighty woman of God? — make us mighty + make us matter — train up.

INTRODUCTION

Though we won't find the younger man's name anywhere in sight, Paul's last letter to Timothy originates in Acts 14. This chapter will be our preoccupation today.

1. We will establish one enormous goal for our series:

mighty _servants_ of God _turned_ _loose_
on _the_ _globe_ in the _Great_ ~~big~~ _name_
of _Jesus_ .

2. Note the NIV wording of Acts 14:1. We are going to ask God from the beginning and throughout our series to blatantly _Ramp_ _up_ ~~over~~ our
effectiveness .
[handwritten] usually effectively

[handwritten] all y'os are called...

How should we communicate our faith?
Christ story
Your story
Our story

A big part of our effectiveness is our _connectedness_ .

Ask questions

have you identified your ministry yet?

Ministry is the collective works God has called us to do in our lifetime upon this planet for __His__ __great__ __glory__.

Faith begins w/ listening

3. Walking with a __whole__ __new__ __level__ of effectiveness __takes__ __faith__.

A launching challenge: Who among us is __willing__ to __believe__ the power of Jesus could __dramatically__ __change__ something that has been __true__ of you __since__ __birth__?

Come live between humble servants of God + know we are mighty women of God

4. We will deal with __erroneous__ __estimates__ of others all __our__ __serving__ __lives__.

Be forewarned: Those __who__ __adore__ can as __quickly__ __abhor__.

5. Five words for the journey:
__just__ __keep__ __getting__ __back__ __up__.

Divine Triangulation

Day One

A TRAIL OF
TWO CITIES

FLASH FORWARD: *Now the time had come ...* LUKE 1:57

The exact year circled the neighborhood of A.D. 30 with a circumference perhaps as wide as A.D. 33. The English word *thereabouts* seems embarrassingly weak-willed to attach to certain historical events of eternal proportions, but this side of the sky we're forced on occasion to embrace it. Our journey begins by wrapping our fingers around that circular band of time and stretching it into a scalene triangle connecting three diverse cities and three very different lives. History has a remarkable way of jumping to life when we give place and face to time. This will be our first task.

Scalene triangle: a triangle with three unequal sides.

FIRST, JERUSALEM. Circle Jerusalem on the map in the margin.

It's half past three in the afternoon in the dead center of the month of Nisan (March-April, according to our calendar). The thick crowd has slowly dispersed. All but one of His closest associates fled early on, most out of fear of guilt by association. Some spectators wandered away in weariness. It takes a long time to watch a person die like that. Perhaps others exited the scene motivated by eeriness, their sandals slapping the rocks with haste amid an ominous midday darkness cloaking the gleaming city of God. In a lightning-quick descent of maddening events, their master, teacher, and miracle worker had been arrested, tried, mocked, slapped, spit upon, and beaten with a blood lust that left Him almost beyond recognition. He was hammered to a cross, gasping for breath for six solid hours until He breathed His last.

And He'd let it happen, too. He'd given Himself over. For years He'd escaped and outwitted His haters. He'd slipped right through crowds. Why didn't He do it this time? He knew He was being betrayed. He'd said it that Thursday night at supper, and yet He went exactly where His betrayer would know to find Him. Like He'd planned it. Like He'd done it on purpose. The kiss of death smacked the face of the Son of God. By the time the sun slid down the warm back of Jerusalem, His body would be stone cold in a hewn tomb, shut tight with a boulder.

SECOND, TARSUS. Circle Tarsus on the map on the previous page, and then draw a line between Tarsus and Jerusalem.

Over 350 miles north of Jerusalem, Hebrews who hadn't made the pilgrimage gathered beneath their roofs by sundown for the high Sabbath of Passover week. They were Jews of the Diaspora scattered far from their ancestral homeland centuries earlier by foreign conquerors and captors. The ground where these Judean seeds took root had not been unkind. The Jews who gathered around Sabbath meals that night were urbanites. This grand city of the Roman province of Cilicia sprouted from the fertile fields at the mouth of the river Cydnus where Alexander the Great once bathed. Fed by the snowy crests of the Taurus mountains north of the city, its crisp river waters spilled into the Mediterranean Sea about a dozen miles south. Hills, fields, a river, and sea: its latitude and longitude marked the map of Asia Minor as a mecca for commercial trade. Tarsus was the celebrated meeting place of Cleopatra and Mark Antony and, by A.D. 30, a land of poets and philosophers. In this city, scholarship was the trophy cheered by spectators and held high in the hands of winners in the competitive game of education. In these pursuits, Tarsus exceeded both Athens and Alexandria according to the ancient Greek geographer Strabo.[1]

The soles of the feet in Tarsus were embedded in what has been called "the heart of the Greco-Roman world."[2] Give that statement pause until that heart gets a pulse. These were bilingual Jews, Hebrew by lineage, covenant, and practice, adapted to Greek and Roman culture. At the risk of overselling the point, they were Jewish by blood and belief, Greek by common language, Roman by rule and, select ones, by citizenship.

A notable young man, about 26 years old in our circle of time, knew his way around that city like the back of his hand. But make no mistake, he would have washed that hand the moment he got home to cleanse himself of unavoidable Gentile smudge. Born and reared on the lush soil of Tarsus, he'd no doubt dipped the sidelocks (Lev. 19:27) of his hair in both the Cydnus and the Great Sea. He'd been a small kid, but a bright one, and from no run-of-the-mill family in the Jewish quarter of the city. His father was a Pharisee and, likely, his father's father, too.

Paul

> Jews in Tarsus were Jewish by blood and belief, Greek by common language, Roman by rule and, select ones, by citizenship.

[margin handwritten notes: in Zechariah 2 it talks about these Jews of exile who chose not to return to Jerusalem]

[margin handwritten note: exile]

[margin handwritten note: education]

PHARISEE. What comes to mind when you hear that word?

"The term 'Pharisee' means 'separated ones.' Perhaps it means that they separated themselves from the masses or that they separated themselves to the study and interpretation of the law. ... They apparently were responsible for the transformation of Judaism from a religion of sacrifice to one of law."[3] Take a moment to let that sentence sink in. Unlike the Sadducees, they shoved a sharp elbow into the stomach of skepticism. "They accepted all the [Old Testament] as authoritative. They affirmed the reality of angels and demons. They had a firm belief in life beyond the grave and a resurrection of the body."[4]

The Pharisees "tended toward political conservatism and religious liberalism. They had developed the oral law as a 'fence around the Torah,' which included detailed interpretations, applications, and amplifications of the written Scriptures to enable people to obey them properly."[5] To Pharisees, the way to God was obedience to the law and yet they "were the progressives of the day, willing to adopt new ideas and adapt the law to new situations."[6]

These insights roll fresh color on the walls of the home where our young man of interest was raised. When his father named him Saul (from the Hebrew *Sha'uwl*, which means *asked for*[7]), few would have pondered why. Saul was the big and bold neon name in the small black print of the ancestral tribe of Benjamin. He was the first crowned head of Israel around 1000 B.C. Never mind that he didn't turn out so well. The Hebrew name was a badge of honor for this up-and-coming urbanite Jew, this native son of Tarsus. His Greco-Roman name was Paulos, meaning *small*. The designation would have no small place later in his life, but in the days his young, yet-to-callus feet clipped those Tarsus streets, it likely meant little more to him than a slight toward his height.

> From what you know of Paul through Acts and his letters, how would you picture him?

According to the earliest physical description on record, Saul was "a man of small stature," but he'd become a towering oak in New Testament history, known to Bible lovers as the apostle Paul. Before we crane our necks upward to the sprawling branches on that tree, we stare downward at his impressive roots.

In this first week, you will see both Saul and Paul used as names for the apostle. Saul was his Hebrew name, while Paul was his Roman name. The first mention of the Roman name is in Acts 13:9, at the beginning of Paul's ministry to the Gentiles.

"The earliest physical description we have of Paul comes from *The Acts of Paul and Thecla*, a second-century apocryphal writing that describes the apostle as 'a man of small stature, with a bald head and crooked legs, in a good state of body, with eyebrows meeting and nose somewhat hooked, full of friendliness; for now he appeared like a man, and now he had the face of an angel.' Although written many years after his death, these words may well reflect an authentic tradition about Paul's actual likeness."[8]

Note the following two-part diagram. The cradle represents Saul's birth and infancy (estimated around A.D. 4). The second image represents him as a grown young man, most likely in his mid- to late-twenties at the time of Christ's crucifixion (around A.D. 30-33).

Search the references underneath the diagram and note every piece of biographical information pertaining to Saul before the crucifixion of Christ. Label each fact below the figures based on where they make the most sense to you in general chronology. In other words, would you relate the information to his birth/infancy (i.e., the city where he was born) or to who Saul had become by his young adulthood? Underline your phrases to indicate facts based on solid Scripture. Leave ample space between the two figures for the additions you will make toward the end of our lesson.

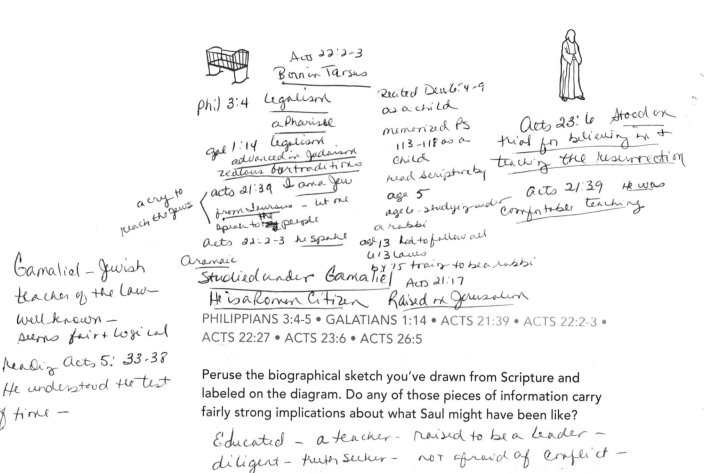

Acts 22:2-3
Born in Tarsus

Phil 3:4 Legalism
a Pharisee

Recited Deut 6:4-9
as a child
memorized PS
113-118 as a
child
read scripture by
age 5
age 6 - studying under
a rabbi
age 13 had to follow all
613 laws
by 15 trains to be a rabbi

Gal 1:14 Legalism
advanced in Judaism
zealous for traditions

acts 21:39 I am a Jew
from Tarsus - let me
speak to the people

Acts 22:2-3 he spoke
Aramaic
Studied under Gamaliel
He is a Roman Citizen

a cry to
reach the Jews

Acts 23:6 Stood on
trial for believing in +
teaching the resurrection

Acts 21:39 He was
comfortable teaching

Acts 21:17
Raised in Jerusalem

Gamaliel - Jewish
teacher of the law -
well known -
seems fair + logical
reading Acts 5: 33-38
He understood the test
of time -

PHILIPPIANS 3:4-5 • GALATIANS 1:14 • ACTS 21:39 • ACTS 22:2-3 •
ACTS 22:27 • ACTS 23:6 • ACTS 26:5

Peruse the biographical sketch you've drawn from Scripture and labeled on the diagram. Do any of those pieces of information carry fairly strong implications about what Saul might have been like?

Educated - a teacher - raised to be a leader -
diligent - truth seeker - not afraid of conflict -

For example, I wore wires on my teeth for 12 years of childhood. From that one biographical fact you could rightly assume my mouth was a mess. But if you further assumed I inherited that gruesome overbite, you'd be mistaken. The truth is, I tripped and fell face-first into a coffee table when running full blast to my big brother when I was five. Drawing reasonable implications from factual information can wrap skin around a skeleton in a character study. Likewise, plausible theories can stick some muscle between the skin and bones and give history's corpse a moment's mobility. Both are valid aspects of a study experience as long as we keep them categorized and don't confuse them with facts.

> With these rules of engagement in mind, if any of Saul's biographical facts on your diagram carry reasonably strong implications, draw a dotted line from them to a blank space in the margin and jot down the possibility followed by a question mark. The dotted line and question mark will differentiate what is theoretical from what you underlined earlier as Scriptural.

Done? Excellent job. Flip back to Acts 22:2-3 and read it once more. Did you catch Paul's reference in verse 3 to "this city" earlier? Follow your fingertip back to Acts 21:17 to identify what city he meant. There you will find the bold line between the first two cities in our triangle of three. There in the Holy City, 355 miles south of Tarsus, Saul's sandals found full traction.

Let's trace the path that took him there. Based on common Jewish practices in an orthodox home around the first century, picture this: Saul would have recited Deuteronomy 6:4-9 before the age the rest of us were in preschool. Through constant repetition of the *Shema*, the Jews reminded themselves of the chief aim of God's chosen people: instruction in the words and ways of *Hashem*, the One they called *The Name*. The little boy, Saul, would soon have begun memorizing Psalms 113–118. By five years of age, he would have begun reading Scripture. By six, he was under a rabbi's instruction in Tarsus. By ten, he was in the classroom throes of oral law. By thirteen, he'd come of age as a son of Israel and was responsible for knowing and living the 613 *mitzvot*, commandments derived from the Hebrew Bible. By fifteen, small Saul was in tall training to become a rabbi.

> Return to your diagram and label these in the space between the cradle and the young man. Omit underlining them since they are not stated clearly in Scripture, but they are well established enough by historians of ancient Jewish tradition to forgo the question marks.

Finished? Okay. We have now arrived at the point when young Saul, around thirteen to fifteen years of age, having advanced far beyond his peers and slacked the jaws of his teachers, transfers to Jerusalem to ultimately study under the most renown rabbi of the day, Gamaliel. This is where we will pick up tomorrow.

> Listen, Israel: The LORD our God, the LORD is One. Love the LORD your God with all your heart, with all your soul, and with all your strength. These words that I am giving you today are to be in your heart. Repeat them to your children. Talk about them when you sit in your house and when you walk along the road, when you lie down and when you get up. Bind them as a sign on your hand and let them be a symbol on your forehead. Write them on the doorposts of your house and on your gates.
>
> DEUTERONOMY 6:4-9

Our own biographies are still underway. They are subtotals—bits and pieces of our stories vulnerable to recalculation with every next ordeal.

Do you feel like yours is under recalculation as you begin this series? *Yes –* If so, in what way?

I need strength – every study that ~~be~~ builds me up will be used by God if I get out ~~the~~ of the way + submit.

Our stories are woven inextricably and often indiscernibly into the thick of our DNA where, to our eyes, the line between what we decided and what was decided for us is a blur. We are a holy collision of the natural and supernatural, sparks constantly flying. We are complicated marvels of genetics, relationships, experience, circumstance, age, education, talent, giftedness, intellect, personality, memory, and physicality. We are dust and spirit handcrafted by a Creator, known and fully understood by Him alone.

So were the men and women on the pages of Scripture. Let's welcome the Holy Spirit to huff and puff warm life into the print and rescue us from thinking complicated thoughts of ourselves while making mannequins of the mortals in Scripture. This process begins for us with a young man named Saul, the bright star of his class, before he'd quite seen the light. So happy you came along.

As you close today, share what brings you to your side of this page.

> We are a holy collision of the natural and supernatural, sparks constantly flying.

On Reading Scripture

During my growing-up years around our house, Mom used to say, "The Bible isn't just any book." I like to think about the ways in which the Bible differs from other books—how it is a book, but how it far surpasses them all too. To me, the Bible is wild and mysterious. As we read Scripture, guided and enlightened by the Holy Spirit, we encounter Jesus Christ. I believe there is real power in engaging this text and that it uniquely energizes us for the work God has given us to do in the world.

Since you and I don't know each other just yet, let me give you a little insight. Sometimes my adult self gives people the impression that I am a "natural student" (their words, not mine—that would be embarrassing!). Although I have, over time, made a decision to dedicate myself to being a lifelong student of Scripture, I don't think it's my nature at all.

I wasn't a bookish kid. I studied for a test at intermittent stoplights while driving to school. Frankly, I preferred higher impact sorts of things. I was the lone girl playing kickball or home-run derby with the squirrelly neighborhood boys. I won the "Miss Fitness" award in fifth grade. Reading wasn't exactly the sport I was looking for. So, to set the record straight, I'm not a natural student at all. I am simply and utterly captivated by the Bible.

It is an absolute testimony to the awesomeness of Scripture that someone who hated Spanish and French as much as I did would spend the past decade learning Greek and Hebrew.

I have a vivid memory of the first time I sat down of my own volition with a Bible. It was during the summer of my fifteenth birthday, on a day when no one else was home except me. I remember the state of my heart that day. I was crushed. And not because someone else had crushed me. I had done something stupid. I realized, as much as my adolescent self could, my own capacity for destruction. I felt completely alone and ashamed. That day, I recalled the words of a verse that is pretty well known to most of us in the church: "You will seek me and find me, when you seek me with all your heart" (Jer. 29:13, ESV). I wrote to God in my journal and told Him that I was seeking, whatever that meant, and I hoped to find Him, if He even existed.

Then I literally just opened up the Bible at random and pointed at a line. My best recollection is that my finger fell on some verses either in Numbers or Deuteronomy because I remember tassels being involved. All I can really say is that during the process of reading those few pages, something happened. I had an encounter with God. N. T. Wright suggests that Scripture "is one of the points where heaven and earth overlap and interlock."[1] That is a beautiful thought, isn't it? In those earliest days, reading the Bible was mostly about me; I had no sophisticated method. And there was a grace for it. At first I didn't really know how the parts fit in with the whole, but I went back for more, time and time again. I felt like the Bible had this mysterious way of reading me and perhaps even changing me. I knew even then that I needed a lot of changing.

Sometimes we read the Bible because we're desperate. We pick up the Psalms and read:

 "If I take the wings of the morning and dwell
 in the uttermost parts of the sea, even there
 your hand shall lead me, and your right hand
 shall hold me" (Ps. 139:9-10, ESV).

Invoking those words with the psalmist helps us get through the day, illuminating the darkness in front of us. But other days we pick up the Scriptures and read with just as much zeal purely because we're part of the Bible's grand narrative. The God we worship is the God of Abraham, Isaac, Jacob, Joseph, Deborah, Isaiah, Jonah, Micah, Mary, Mary Magdalene, Jesus, Paul, Junia, Phoebe, and John, the beloved disciple. When we engage this book we begin to lift up our eyes and gaze at something cosmic God is doing that surpasses our own generation. His work of redemption and renewal spans centuries and civilizations. When we read this text, we are called to play our part in the drama of redemption.

It's worth stating that Christians don't worship the Bible by any means, but we believe there is tremendous power in it. We believe it is the revelation of God. We read the Bible because we need an encounter with God; we need to hear His words. These days we are always reading words—scrolling Twitter, reading emails, text messages, and the pretty Instagram quotes. We want quick inspiration. Reading Scripture, however, is slower, quieter work. It takes time, patience, and attention, but if we're looking to nourish our souls, nothing can compete with it.

Not long ago I was at a retreat where a well-known poet challenged us to memorize poems. Someone in the crowd asked him to explain why. He said, "So you will have them when you need them." I get that. I feel the same way about Scripture. I am not talking about memorizing Scripture, but reading it. Really reading it. More importantly, allowing it to read us. Sometimes we don't know Scripture has taken root in us until we realize, in light of a particular circumstance, it was there, written on our hearts, preparing us to navigate the moment. That particular word was alive in us and changed the way we acted or reacted in that impossible situation. It brought us hope in a moment of soul-shaking despair. We were also able to pass it along to someone else who needed it. And it impacts us in more subtle ways, too. We find we're more content and satisfied than we were before, though our circumstances haven't improved at all.

We are encountering Jesus when we read this text and over time, despite what we originally thought, we are making it; the Word of God is sustaining us.

Day Two

MEET THE TEACHER

FLASH FORWARD: *I am a Jewish man, born in Tarsus of Cilicia but brought up in this city at the feet of Gamaliel and educated according to the strict view of our patriarchal law. Being zealous for God, just as all of you are today.* ACTS 22:3

We've dedicated Week One to constructing a scalene triangle between three different cities to connect three different lives in one loose circle of time.

How many cities have we accrued so far? __2__

By the end of Day One, we established the first link between them. What was it? *Paul was born in Taursus + as a teen studied to be a Pharisee in Jerusalem*

I've steered you wrong if I've left you picturing Saul's entire childhood consumed with religious training. Jewish fathers were also responsible for teaching their sons a viable trade to earn a living. To do otherwise, according to an ancient Jewish saying, was to train his son to be a thief.[9]

ACTS 18:3 PEGS SAUL'S TRADE. (Forgive me. I can't resist a pun to save my life.) What was his trade? *Tent maker*

Tarsus was known all over Asia Minor for tents composed of ebony hides and woven coats of long-haired goats native to the Taurus mountains. Saul's tent making was fund-raising to support what he loved most. And what Saul loved most was studying, articulating, interpreting, reciting, instructing, and debating the Hebrew Scriptures and oral traditions. A prodigy of rumination, he could gnaw a scroll like a bone.

The eyes of the pupil would have been wide with wonder the first day of class with the great Gamaliel. The name of this acclaimed rabbi shows up twice in the New Testament, both times in the Book of Acts (5:34; 22:3). We saw the latter reference in our previous lesson straight from Paul's own mouth. Glance up at today's Flash Forward for a reminder. Let's camp on the first reference to him in Acts 5:34. For now, please read the one verse only, and, after we take a moment to applaud it, we'll go back and consider the context.

What can you unearth about Gamaliel from Acts 5:34 alone?

He was well respected by Paul & the Sanhedrin — like when they were willing to listen & be led by Gamaliel — if he spoke they listen — EF Hutton talks people listen

If your translation speaks of Gamaliel serving "in the council" but does not identify which one, the phrase refers to the Sanhedrin. Comprised of 71 elite men and chaired by the high priest, the Sanhedrin was the preeminent Jewish council in the first century A.D.[10] That is an impressive pedigree, but the implication of his inclusion on the council throws Gamaliel into a league of his own: "The Sanhedrin included both of the main Jewish parties among its membership. Since the high priest presided, the Sadducean priestly party seems to have predominated, but some leading Pharisees also were members (Acts 5:34; 23:1-9)."[11]

Circle the minority party in the previous quote. Was Gamaliel a Sadducee or a Pharisee? *Pharisee*

According to Acts 5:34, which group held him in high esteem?

honored by all

God be praised. Somebody put down your pen and give the man a hand. Throw some confetti. Gamaliel somehow managed to be respected by two completely different parties notoriously prone, as leaders often are, to rabid competition. We could use some Gamaliels on our religious landscape today and some prominent leaders with enough security and humility to honor one another even on different sides of issues.

Social media has done an embarrassingly good job of capturing the snarling face of Christian sectarianism on camera. Worse yet, it holds a megaphone to its mouth. Few of us would argue against the right to practice faith and closest fellowship in churches where we're most comfortable doctrinally or even stylistically in worship. Further, a belief system that will not tolerate respectful debate and disagreement within its ranks is terrifying. Rebuke can even be godly, but, according to Jesus, a public rebuke was the last resort, not the first retort, and was primarily for issues of sin, not variance of stands (Matt. 18:17). We are unspeakably privileged in our culture to have the microphone of social media put to our mouths to spread the gospel and great love of Jesus Christ. But many of our parties—I wish I meant the dancing kind—are so publicly slanderous of one another that we've compromised our

> A belief system that will not tolerate respectful debate and disagreement within its ranks is terrifying.

entrusted

credibility and cut the legs out from under our table of fellowship. You and I could be part of propping that table back up. We don't have to have matching plates to sit at the same table as long as Christ is seated at the head. I tend to like having a person next to me with something different on her plate. Don't you? If we stare at it long enough, she might offer us a bite and who knows? We might come to appreciate a whole new taste at the broad and beautiful table of Jesus. If, on the other hand, something doesn't taste right on her plate, we'll know to keep our fork out of it.

Now let's widen the lens to the context around the first mention of Gamaliel.

READ ACTS 5:12-42. The segment isn't short but it's rich. Once you've read it, complete the following:

Who were the people arrested, imprisoned, and then threatened again by the Sanhedrin? *The Apostles*

What had they been strictly charged not to do (v. 28?)
Teach about Jesus

What was their response in verse 29?
Obey God

Peter, in effect, switched sides of the courtroom and issued a countercharge to the Sanhedrin in verse 30. What was it?
You killed Jesus

How did the council react according to verse 33?
Furious + wanted to kill the Apostles

NOW FOCUS ENTIRELY UPON GAMALIEL. Review Acts 5:34-39. On a scale of 1 to 10, how would you score his extemporaneous speech?
10 - wise - not just smart but wise -

How did he build his case with the council members in verses 35-37?
He brought up previous examples (very lawyery of him) of leaders + movements that came + went

In your own words, what was Gamaliel's counsel to his colleagues in verses 38-39?
Let this movement go - if it dies out so be it - if it grows + thrives it is of God - don't fight God -

The Q & A's you see sprinkled throughout the study were generated from a blog that I posted for the sake of gaining insight right before we taped the sessions. Here was my request: *Think about what you wish you and I could talk about if we could grab a Starbucks® together. Form it into a clear question and present it in a succinct blog comment to this post.* I was overwhelmed with the response. Praying you will be encouraged by these brief conversations.

Q & A

Carmen: *What's been the hardest thing for you to let go of?*

Beth: *For many grueling years, the hardest thing for me to let go of was regret. I fixated on how deeply I regretted certain terribly consequential decisions in my past and I could not stop grieving my foolishness. My regret lingered many years beyond genuine repentance and finally became so oppressive that I begged Jesus to deliver me. It has been a lengthy process but I'm deeply grateful to no longer be in bondage to it.*

Do you know a man you could picture in Gamaliel's shoes? A man with both courageous and careful speech who is respected even by those on opposing sides of multiple issues? Or, as a second option, if this were a scene in a movie, what actor would you handpick to play Gamaliel's role? Answer either question or both as a reminder that Gamaliel was not faceless.

Albert — I picture Albert. He is educated + a great teacher — He has lived a varied life + sees things from many angles + then uses his wisdom to help us understand both sides — before Christ in his life + after Christ in his life.

Gamaliel's voice wasn't generic. It had pitch and cadence. His heart thundered in his chest as he stood to his feet and took command of the room. The hero in this scene was Saul's teacher. Saul sat at those very feet. Store that fact somewhere for keeps.

The events in Acts 5 take place before we are introduced to Saul but certainly not before he'd come to Jerusalem to sit under the teaching of Gamaliel. Keep in mind throughout our series that Saul and Jesus were contemporaries, though of very different geographical origins. Jesus was born in Bethlehem and raised in Nazareth, a small town in the hill country of Galilee hundreds of miles south of Tarsus. However, like most devout Jewish households in Israel, His family would have traveled to Jerusalem multiple times.

Keep in mind throughout our series that Saul and Jesus were contemporaries, though of very different geographical origins.

> CHECK EXODUS 23:14-17. How often were the men of Israel summoned to "appear before the Lord GOD"? *3*

List the occasions below. (And, if you were the kid in high school who couldn't resist the extra credit assignment, you can easily find out online what times of year those occasions occurred. If you do so, record them as well.)

The month of Nissan is the 1st month on the Jewish Calendar + it is our Springtime

- *Festival of Unleavened Bread - 7 days - duration of Passover all yeast needed removal from the house - Spring is 2020 april 8-16*
- *Festival of Harvest - first fruits - Summer - Early June - for 2019 June 8-10*
- *Festival of Ingathering - crop gathering - also called Festival of Tabernacles - Celebrated 15th day of the 7th month - 10/14/19 this year*

our October is their 7th month

These were the pilgrimage feasts and, once God established one city for His name and circled it with a crown, to "appear before the Lord GOD" (v. 17) meant showing up in Jerusalem.

Saul was younger than Jesus, perhaps by seven or eight years, but their age gap is no wider than that of many brothers. According to Acts 22:3, Saul was "brought up in [Jerusalem] at the feet of Gamaliel" and "educated" there. He would have been within those city walls for a number of years, at the very least throughout his rabbinical training. Later in the Book of Acts, his nephew is referenced in Jerusalem (23:16). Think how many times Jesus and Saul may have been within the same city walls at the same exact time. Don't you find the thought fascinating? It piques my curiosity in all sorts of ways.

Does it rattle up any questions in your bones? List a few.

Saul may not have known Jesus – But Jesus for sure knew Saul / Paul + what he would become in history. As a human I would have wanted to meet Paul – or look in on him – but we see no mention in the Bible of such a thing.

I often wonder what Pauls position on all of his Christian life would have been had he been part of the Sanhedrin or near that position when Christ was crucified

Keep that curiosity of yours kicking up dust until our next lesson. Under the teaching of Rabbi Jesus, curiosity is the shovel that turns an everyday class into an archaeological dig and it's the canvas that turns a black and white scroll into a kaleidoscope. In Matthew 7:7-8, Jesus said, "Keep asking, and it will be given to you. Keep searching, and you will find. Keep knocking, and the door will be opened to you. For everyone who asks receives, and the one who searches finds, and to the one who knocks, the door will be opened." Here's the thing. You will not always find the answer to your question but you will find the better treasure God buried where He knew your curiosity would send you searching. Embrace the mystery.

> All the treasures of wisdom and knowledge are hidden in Him.
>
> COLOSSIANS 2:3

Day Three

WHERE WAS HE WHEN

FLASH FORWARD: *For I didn't think it was a good idea to know anything among you except Jesus Christ and Him crucified.* 1 CORINTHIANS 2:2

Where were you when ___9/11 hit___?
Every generation gasping for air right now can fill in that blank several times over with events big enough to be known by anyone paying a whit of attention to world news. For my parents' generation, the blank was filled first by the assassination of John F. Kennedy in 1963 and, second, by Neil Armstrong's left foot stepping off the ladder of Apollo 11 and onto the moon. The year was 1969.

My generation's coming of age could fill the blank with Nixon's resignation over Watergate in 1974 and the death of Elvis Presley in 1977.

My firstborn, Amanda, and her friend Jenny were standing in front of our television in 1986 waiting for the afternoon kindergarten bus when a special report bellowed the news of the Challenger Space Shuttle explosion. I snatched the children into the kitchen and then stood in horror as the screen captured white ribbons of smoke curling like monstrous antennae against a cerulean sky. Eleven years later, I was in New Orleans in a convenience store parking lot on my way to speak at a church when news came over the radio that Princess Di was dead. You also remember exactly where you were when certain world-news events took place. Maybe it was 9/11 or the Boston Marathon Bombing. Whatever the event, that moment is cemented in your memory.

> Go back to the question that began our lesson and fill in the blank with your most prominent example, and then answer the completed question in the margin. Add a second example and your whereabouts below it.

The popular unifier *where were you when?* didn't originate in the 20th century era of broadcast news. Actually, the Bible posed it first in what many scholars believe could well be its oldest book.

At Walmart stand ~

entrusted

Look up Job 38:4. Who asked the question, who was addressed, and what was the occasion for the "where were you when"?

God asked Job - where were you when the Earth was formed -

The glaring event that filled in the blank for the early church took place on a hill outside Jerusalem circa A.D. 30. The completed question: Where were you when Jesus was crucified?

That was hands-down my most pressing question for Saul of Tarsus at the end of our previous lesson. Did it make your list? So, where was Saul when Jesus was crucified? Was he in Jerusalem where Jesus was accused, tried, and condemned, then crucified just outside the city? Scripture offers no definitive answer. Therefore, at the end of this lesson and this lifetime, we still won't know, but let's follow a few trails and think in terms of likelihood.

We'll start with the yes-spectrum among scholars and theologians. Their views range all the way from "*of course* Saul was in Jerusalem when Jesus was crucified" to "most likely the man was in Jerusalem when Jesus was crucified." Saul's own testimony of his lifestyle prior to his encounter with Christ offers substantial support for the yes-spectrum. As we documented on Day Two, he'd been "a Hebrew of Hebrews" (Phil. 3:5), a Pharisee, and a strict adherent of the law who'd made Jerusalem his second home. His practices after his conversion weigh heavily as well.

READ ACTS 20:16 FOR A PRIME EXAMPLE. Why didn't he stay in Ephesus?

To get to Jerusalem for Passover -
So even after he found Christ he respected + even treasured the traditions of his ancestors - Very respectful + important to reach Jews for Christ

The New King James rendering of Acts 18:20-21 is often cited as major support for the yes-spectrum: "When they asked him to stay a longer time with them, he did not consent, but took leave of them, saying, 'I must by all means keep this coming feast in Jerusalem; but I will return again to you, God willing'" (NKJV). And he sailed from Ephesus.

So it would have been this same during the Passover when Jesus was murdered

The Feast of Harvest in Exodus 23:16 is also called both the Feast of Weeks and Pentecost.

If he still longed to keep the feasts in Jerusalem after his conversion when he was no longer bound to the law, imagine his devotion prior to his conversion when a Pharisee's adherence was paramount.

The question currently on the table is whether Saul was in Jerusalem at the time of Jesus' death. The crucifixion of Christ took place during the Passover event. The Passover, also known as the Feast of Unleavened Bread, was the most prominent pilgrimage feast of all. For this reason, we could lean toward a yes.

Now let's back up to our starting point and take the other trail in support of the no-spectrum. Search the verses below and document both the occasion and the location mentioned either by Paul (post-conversion Saul) or in reference to him.

REFERENCE	OCCASION	PAUL'S LOCATION
Acts 20:5-6	Passover week or Fest. of Unleavened Bread	Troas
1 Corinthians 16:8-9	Pentacost	Ephesus

Both of these feasts followed Saul's conversion to Christ so they aren't airtight evidences to support the possibility that Saul was away from Jerusalem on Passover circa A.D. 30. They do suggest, however, that, if he could not be in Jerusalem at the time of the feasts, his practice was to observe them wherever he was. This might not have been out of the box for him even prior to his encounter with Jesus.

Glance back at Day One to record the distance between Tarsus and Jerusalem. 350 miles

exiled

Diaspora Jews planted woefully far from Jerusalem soil still practiced the grueling pilgrimage (Acts 2:9-11), but sometimes circumstances forced devotees to observe the feasts in their local communities. Was Saul perhaps back in Tarsus when the violent stir broke out in the city of God over Jesus? Or could he have been elsewhere?

I'll tell you why I'm probing. If Saul was in Jerusalem at the time of the trial, the public flogging, and the crucifixion, why didn't he make reference to being there in the copious ink of 13 letters or in one of his addresses recorded in Acts? Even if he'd somehow managed to be in the city and remain oblivious to it—a thought highly unlikely for a Pharisee of his caliber—why didn't he tell on himself? After his conversion, he was fixated on the cross of Christ.

Paul certainly made mention of witnessing Stephen's martyrdom (Acts 22:20).

What did he say to the Corinthians in 1 Corinthians 2:2?
That he came to them to preach only Jesus — nothing else

And rightly so. Faith in Christ's work on the cross was and still remains our single saving grace. No voice in Scripture more loudly proclaims the gospel than Paul's, yet he never mentioned being in Jerusalem the afternoon the crucifixion occurred. His time line doesn't start circling like a vulture around the name of Jesus until Acts 7:58–8:3.

> Read these six verses and record the events surrounding the first mention of Saul.

[handwritten, left margin: Paul was apt 27 at this time at 27 I was inexperienced but thought I knew about some of my activities + opinions, I am embarrassed by some of my 27 yr old activities + opinions. was Paul?]

[handwritten response: The Sanhedrin was stoning Stephen for proclaiming the Gospel + Saul/Paul held their garments (why didn't he join in?) Saul worked at destroying the church going door to door to drag off men + women to imprison them for being Christians!]

> Now, glance at the next mention of him in Acts 9:1-2 and record his activities.

[handwritten response: He was actively + aggressively trying to persecute Christians – asked permission + authority to go to Damascus to chase down Christians — Question why didn't Paul get the Jerusalem apostles arrested??]

Wait a second. Do these sound to you like the actions of a devout student of the Rabbi Gamaliel whose cool head simmered down the entire Sanhedrin and spared the apostles' lives? Me either. Let me throw something out to you that I found fascinating. By the time Saul came of age as a young Pharisee, lines within the sect were drawn sharply between two dominant schools of thought: the Hillelites and the Shammaites. Hillel and Shammai were the two most influential teachers in Pharisaism during the reign of Herod the Great, just one generation prior to Saul's. In documentations in the Jewish Mishnah compiled around A.D. 200, "almost always Hillel is the 'lenient' one, and Shammai is the 'strict' one."[12]

If you're sufficiently caffeinated, you might jump to the same conclusion I would have: clearly, Saul was a Shammaite. But this is where the plot thickens. If he was, he bucked the ranks of his own primary teacher. Gamaliel was Hillel's grandson. That Gamaliel was a chip off the moderate old block is evident in his address to the Sanhedrin. It was Hillel who said, "That which is hateful to you, do not do to your fellow. That is the whole Torah; the rest is the explanation. Now go and learn."[13] His school of thought, "broadly speaking, pursued a policy of 'live and let live.' Let the Herods and the Pilates … rule the world—let them even rule Israel, politically—just as long as we Jews are allowed to study and practice Torah (the Jewish law) in peace. The Shammaites believed this wasn't good enough."[14]

[handwritten, right margin: That sounds like Jesus = love your neighbor as yourself – Did he learn from Hillel or Gamaliel as well?]

So don't bother picturing Gamaliel's feet beside Saul's where garments of those stoning Stephen were stacked. Don't envision the face of the teacher nodding in tandem approval with his student's as Stephen's flesh was pummeled crimson and purple. The zeal that drove Saul of Tarsus to soon burst through doors, breathing threats and murder (Acts 9:1), to drag men and women to prison wasn't lit by the lamp on Gamaliel's desk. How on earth was the wick lit? All is conjecture but Saul wouldn't be the first hot-blooded student to cast off a gentle mentor's mantle at the first blush of revolution.

In his later testimonials, he makes no mention of being in Jerusalem at the time of the crucifixion, yet, soon after, he is a leader of the pack in the persecution. All we can offer the silence is a scribbling theory, but Saul seems to me like a man making up for lost time. Like a man making up for the embarrassing transgression of missing out, perhaps, on the biggest story to hit Jerusalem in circa A.D. 30. His fellow Pharisees in the city would have been neck deep in the fray and maybe it wouldn't have been such a big deal had it fizzled out. But then those rumors spread like a plague that the blasphemer's body was missing from the tomb and, by Pentecost, the menacing handful following The Way had multiplied into thousands. No way were they getting away with that. Not on Saul's watch.

On the high road of that rabid zeal we land our lesson. Read Acts 9:1-9 and, if you've read it many times, try to read it with new eyes. If you're like me, some responsive thoughts are rolling around in your head as you raise your chin from that page. Record two of them as your conclusion today:

1. why did Saul hate People of the Way so so much?

2. why did God choose Saul for this job & not say — Barnabas or Timothy or any of the other followers?

Last of all, as to one ripped from the womb, he appeared even to me.
1 CORINTHIANS 15:8[15]

entrusted

Day Four

A BEELINE TO CITY THREE

FLASH FORWARD: *Then he went on to Derbe and Lystra, where there was a disciple named Timothy, the son of a believing Jewish woman, but his father was a Greek.* **ACTS 16:1**

We've devoted our first week of study to a circle of time around A.D. 30 stretched into a scalene triangle connecting three cities and three key lives. Our first stop was Jerusalem where Jesus of Nazareth had been arrested, tried, and, His back whipped to shreds, forced to carry a criminal's cross outside the city walls. Nailed to that wood in public view for six gruesome hours, He'd just taken His last breath as we opened Day One. We then set our GPS 355 miles north to Asia Minor where we parked in Tarsus, the hometown of a brilliant young student of the Jewish dispersion named Saul, approximately seven years younger than Jesus. Surpassing his peers, Saul relocated to Jerusalem for an aspiring rabbi's Ivy League equivalent. During the years of Saul's study, the Galilean family of Jesus would have traversed in and out of the city on pilgrimage.

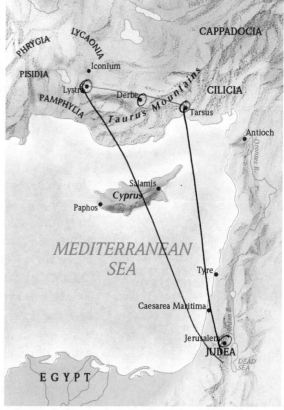

Fill in the names of our first two cities accordingly.

First, _Jerusalem_

Second, _Taursus_

Today we draw a line to the final city in our divine triangulation and establish the connection between the three lives that drive our five-week study. Travel north again from Jerusalem to Tarsus on your map. From Tarsus, head west, veering slightly northward through the Roman province of Cilicia into the region of Lycaonia in the province of Galatia. You'll need to hike over the Taurus mountains as part of your journey. Close to the 90-mile marker, you can stop in Derbe for a cup of good, strong *Türk kahvesi* (Turkish coffee) to shake your drowsiness. With the last sip, you hit the road, setting your sights about 35 miles northwest to your final destination, the city of Lystra.

Fill the name of the city in the blank:

third, _Lystra_____.

In Lystra, you're looking for the home of Eunice. You can't assume you'll find it in the Jewish quarter of Lystra like you could have found Saul's residence in Tarsus. Eunice married a Gentile. To what degree this broke the heart of her mother, Lois, remains unknown to us, but to the elder woman's credit, she did not shun her. Whether or not most Diaspora Jews in Lystra responded in kind also remains a mystery. If they were devout law-keepers, Eunice was, at best, coolly treated for her compromise. By the time a gust of wind on her way to market could betray her rounded tummy, she was one midwife away from the biggest complication of her eclectic wedding vows.

> They called the little guy Timothy, "a personal name meaning 'honoring God.'"

It was a boy. They called the little guy Timothy, "a personal name meaning 'honoring God.'"[17] In the event you're smiling, I am, too. I love that Eunice might have hoped against hope he'd have a fighting chance to honor God despite coming from a union thought to dishonor Him.

This slice of information will find a significant place in Timothy's biography: "The marriage of a Jewish woman to a non-Jew was considered a nonlegal marriage; and in all instances of nonlegal marriages, the lineage of the child was reckoned through the mother."[18]

Not the dad. The mom.

> **READ GENESIS 17:9-14.** What would have been the first step of obedience for a boy counted in the lineage of Abraham?
>
> _Circumcision_
>
> How serious was this command? Explain.
>
> _If any male was not circumcised he would be cut off from the his people — shunned — considered dead_

Store that information and we'll loop back to it on Day Five.

The traditional date of Timothy's birth was A.D. 17. However, if recent estimates of many Bible scholars are more accurate about Timothy's age at certain key events in his story, he was born closer to our circle of time (A.D. 30-33). We will do the math in tomorrow's lesson. Whether Timothy was a newborn, a young child, or not quite yet conceived, his mother would have been completely unaware of the spotless Lamb of God slain for the sins of the world in Jerusalem that fated Passover. All of us to one degree or another are, at first, oblivious to the fact that, one afternoon just outside the holy city, a sinless Savior gave His life, covering us under a blanket of blood to save our lives and cloak us in white.

She would not remain oblivious, nor would her son. If you joined us for our first video session, we've explored the events in Paul's initial missionary journey that first exposed Timothy and Eunice to the gospel of Christ. If not, please take a moment to read Acts 14:1-22. If you are already familiar with Paul's first journey to Lystra, proceed straight ahead to Acts 15:36–16:5 and complete the following:

So Timothy was not circumcised at 8 days old—

> What happened to a team of gospel laborers in Acts 15:37-39 and why?

They had a disagreement + parted ways.
Barnabas + Paul parted company

> **REWIND PAUL'S STORY TO SHORTLY AFTER HIS CONVERSION BY READING ACTS 9:26-27.** What significant part did Barnabas play?

He was the bridge between Saul/Paul + the apostles — he vouched for Paul

> **READ ACTS 13:1-3.** How did the two men end up officially serving together?

Holy Spirit appointed them — the believers laid hands on them prayed for them. It was a divine-holy assignment

Two immensely devoted servants of Jesus, godly men, who'd shared miles of territory, thousands of conversations, innumerable joys, harrowing close calls, near-deaths, divine wonders, and God only knows how many hours in prayer, suddenly shot apart like shrapnel in an explosive argument. Through the power of the living Christ, they'd scaled insurmountable obstacles elbow-to-elbow but they couldn't survive disparity over the cousin of Barnabas (Col. 4:10). One of the baffling elements of human relationships is how little it can take to plummet from such a hard-earned, fought-for summit. We stuck together through all of that and we're going to fall apart over this? I have a strong feeling you can relate on some level to what happened between Paul and Barnabas. I can, too.

Sharp disagreement is the English translation of the Greek *paroxysmos* (Acts 15:39).

> Share your story. *missy —*

> If you haven't done so in your previous answer, focus specifically on how one of your own relationships was compromised by differences of opinion on a third person. Share to the degree you feel comfortable.

Make that third person your own flesh and blood and the stakes shoot sky high. I don't know about you but I'm grateful God saw fit to weave this part of their story into the fabric of Scripture because torn relationships happen to us, too, and they are deeply painful. We'd like to think mutual love for Jesus inoculates us against a falling out of this sort, but we are still so vulnerably human. Scripture never says who was right or wrong in this case. Perhaps God took neither side. That's the beauty of the cross anyway. No human ax can split its wood. Even when flesh tears, Jesus is indivisible and seamless, like the tunic snatched by the soldiers who crucified Him. He can be grieved but He can't be ripped to shreds by relationships and parceled piecemeal between

We'd like to think mutual love for Jesus inoculates us against a falling out of this sort, but we are still so vulnerably human.

two parties. No judge on earth can limit His visitation rights. Where He goes, He goes in one piece. He is always and only whole. That day when Barnabas and Mark sailed away to Cyprus, Christ went fully with them. And, when Paul and Silas departed, He also went wholly with them.

> Check your map on the inside back cover and record which directions on a compass Barnabas and Paul went (Acts 15:39-41).
> Barnabas: *SE*
> Paul: *E and then S.*

If an indivisible Savior on an indestructible cross is the beauty in the ugliness of division, this is surely the redemption: what flesh had divided, the Spirit multiplied. One ministry team turned into two. You and I both know it doesn't always happen that way. It takes cooperation. We can stunt God's redemptive work in our midst with our bitterness, unforgiveness, slander, blame, chronic regret, and unresolved guilt. Or we can go face down and beg God in our fractures to do something bigger with the broken pieces than He might have done with the whole.

We're left to wonder all sorts of things. How long did Paul and Barnabas harbor negative emotions? How did each process the breakage? Did one talk incessantly about it to anyone who'd listen? Did the other refuse to speak of it, almost like none of it ever happened? Did observers take sides? Did Paul and Barnabas miss one another or were they each easily replaced?

> In our yearnings for significance and some semblance of uniqueness, none of us wants to feel easily replaced. Have you ever felt that you were? If so, share as much as you are willing in the margin.

Humans are not one-size-fits-all.

Humans are not one-size-fits-all. For one human being to perfectly replace another, leaving no lacks, gaps, or empty edges, somebody gets dehumanized. Only compromised hearts are no worse for the wear in the wake of relational carnage. Healthy skin scars when it's torn. That's the way we were made. The wonder of long-term relationships is that fragile pieces prone to part instead hold fast. Don't take them for granted. Marvel over the miracle of long-time loves and friendships. I write these words with a very tender heart the day after my thirty-seventh wedding anniversary.

We have no facts to fill in the blanks of Acts 15:39 but we may have one little hint that speaks above a whisper. The hole Barnabas left in the life of Paul was so deep, so wide, it left room enough for two: Silas and a young half-breed named Timothy.

Theology: A Collective Struggle

Whether you're joining us with a group or going solo with this study, I'm happy you're here. In my first article I shared a bit about my experience reading Scripture. The time I spend alone reading Scripture is sacred to me and essential to my life. I intend for it to stay that way until the day I die. But intellectual community is also necessary for me. I need people who will talk with me about the theological ideas I am processing and who will share with me the ideas they're processing, too. I need people who will theologically wrestle with me and disagree with me and push me to see things from a different perspective. I need people to affirm that my thoughts aren't insane or heretical or just plain silly. Thanks be to God, I have a few of these people in my life. I can honestly say that Mom is my primary dialogue partner. When we're together we usually talk Bible and theology at some point and we are together often. Also, it's common to receive a text from her by 7:30 a.m. that says something like, "I can't wait to tell you what I am learning about the Widow of Nain!"

In 2012, while reading Benjamin Myers' excellent book on the theology of Rowan Williams, I came across these unforgettable sentences:

"Theology ... is not a private table for one but a rowdy banquet of those who gather, famished and thirsty, around Christ. The lonely work of reading and writing is not yet theology but only its preparation. Theology happens wherever we are drawn together into the congenial and annoying labour of conversing, listening, and disputing—in short, where we are drawn into a collective struggle for truthful speech."[2]

When I read those words for the first time, I must have sighed loudly enough for everyone in my building to hear.

Studying is necessary but the theological task is not complete until our private readings have joined "a collective struggle for truthful speech."

And this struggle involves all of us who are united in Christ. Theology is not just for the guy with the theology degree who wears tweed and smokes a cigar. You, yes you, are part of this process. You don't have to do all the talking, but your voice needs to be heard. You might not get all the jargon yet but you need to enter the conversation. We need the teachers, yes, but we need the beginners, too, and everyone in between.

You know, we may especially need the beginners. For people like me, who were exposed to Scripture from infancy, there is a danger of over-familiarity. Too often we assume we already know what the Bible says or means. Or, we are so familiar with certain language that we simply stop noticing its beauty. George Milligan said it best: "We know how our very familiarity with Scriptural language is apt to blind us to its full significance."[3] One of the best examples of this is the word *gospel*. A lot of us have heard this word our whole lives but we could not coherently explain its true meaning to someone if they paid us to.

Frequently a new reader of the Bible is able to point out something we have never seen before about the most common word or phrase.

Many people I know, women in particular, are suspicious of theological conversation. Mean-spirited people who use Scripture as a weapon have turned off a lot of us at some point along the way. Most of us know "that guy." You know, the one who stands in line after Sunday's sermon with his Greek New Testament delightfully waiting to show the preacher where he got it dreadfully wrong. This sort of thing has understandably made us a little shy about or disinterested in theological conversation. But there is a better way to discuss theology and that better way is usually around a table. That's why I so appreciate these words:

"We don't come to the table to fight or to defend. We don't come to prove or to conquer, to draw lines in the sand or to stir up trouble. We come to the table because our hunger brings us there. We come with a need, with fragility, with an admission of our humanity. The table is the great equalizer, the level playing field many of us have been looking everywhere for. The table is the place where the doing stops, the trying stops, the masks are removed, and we allow ourselves to be nourished, like children. We allow someone else to meet our need. In a world that prides people on not having needs, on going longer and faster, on going without, on powering through, the table is a place of safety and rest and humanity, where we are allowed to be as fragile as we feel. If the home is a body, the table is the heart, the beating center, the sustainer of life and health."[4]

This is the kind of place we need when we're talking about ideas that really matter to us. Some people don't believe in talking religion or politics at the table, but what better place would there be as long as the people at the table are mutually dedicated to a posture of humility? Part of caring about something deeply is opening oneself up to vulnerability.

One of my best memories from Bible study comes from a few years ago when I was in a group of about ten. It's not a coincidence that we all gathered in a breakfast room around a big farm table covered with easy casual food and coffee mugs. I was co-leading the group with a friend and one of the girls in our group disagreed with most everything I suggested. This caused some awkward moments. If my position was far right, she was far left, or vice versa, on whatever subject we were discussing. She didn't disagree with me just to be argumentative. She had her reasons. But she cared enough about the material to talk about it. I grew to greatly appreciate her as she often pushed me to my intellectual limits. Sometimes I ended up moving closer to her perspective and other times I ended up disagreeing with her even more firmly, refining and solidifying my initial arguments. In the end, she made me a better reader of the Bible. I think of her often and fondly. I am not really suggesting that all of our Bible study groups should meet around a dinner table, though I am glad some of them do.

Mostly I just hope you have a few human beings you can be vulnerable with, process with, talk eye to eye with about Scripture, theology, and ideas that matter to you most without fear of ridicule or rejection. I find that I do that best with my people around a table.

Day Five

A NEW SON AND A CIRCUMCISION

FLASH FORWARD: *But you know his proven character, because he has served with me in the gospel ministry like a son with a father.* **PHILIPPIANS 2:22**

Like you perhaps, I'm a thinker. Well, maybe I'm more of an over-thinker. In fact, if life is going too fast and I don't get time to myself to mull over recent events or conversations or shared experiences, where they fit and if and how they have meaning, I start getting grouchy. It's the meditation that brings home the satisfaction to me. An experience is left hanging until I've gathered it up in my thoughts, mulled it over, then laid it, if it begs a place, on an open page of Scripture.

I've come to believe there is a divine plan, an orchestration of events, opportunities, and encounters, not only historically and eschatologically regarding the people of God but for each person of God individually. In the blinding ambush of the present, so much that happens in our lives seems random. However, retrospect helps us see those happenings through the lens of order, which may reveal something shocking. Ink splotches start to form edges and the edges start to look like puzzle pieces, and, lo and behold, a handful of them actually fit. It's far from a comprehensive landscape, but often all it takes for us to hang in there is the merest hint that something means something.

I often think about what I would have missed had my path been one straight line from A to B and B to C, rather than a sharp turn here and a soft veer there. With every curve and corner God was sketching unforeseen triangles between Jesus, me, and a handful of unrelated others. Second only to Scripture, God has used and continues to use key people to shape the phases of my calling. Key, not because they're superior to others, but because God uses them to unlock something in me that proves crucial or stunningly directional in the next season. Don't miss the present tense in the phrase *continues to use.* Callings are organic just like the people God uses to invest in them. To decide at 25 that we know exactly what this thing is supposed to look like is to set ourselves up for failure, faithlessness, and boredom and to miss some of the most meaningful relationships of our lives. Don't fix your feet in concrete. Keep moving and savor the fellow sojourners God deposits along your path, remembering to look back every now and then. A purposeful glance in the rearview mirror will clearly show how desperately we needed what somebody brought us.

To decide at 25 that we know exactly what this thing is supposed to look like is to set ourselves up for failure, faithlessness, and boredom and to miss some of the most meaningful relationships of our lives.

So, what does all this mulling-over have to do with Jesus, Paul, and Timothy? Well, everything. What if Paul had shut down after the falling out with Barnabas? Or, what if he'd decided to keep everything strictly professional and to forgo all things personal? What if he'd bought into staying ahead of the game by withholding his heart? Or what if he'd played "tick tock, the game is locked" and refused to make room in his life for anyone new? Or, what if he'd decided Silas was the only companion he needed? Or—humor me here a moment—what if Silas had gotten all pouty and jealous and Paul had pandered to the codependency?

> **READ PHILIPPIANS 2:19-24 CAREFULLY.** List exactly what Paul would have missed.

What if the next person on your path is meant to become one of the most important people in your entire journey? One of the very dearest? Most influential? What if he or she is the extension of God's index finger pointing you that way? Here's the scary part: the biggest obstacle we have to our next relationship may well be our previous relationship. This could be true whether our last relationship proved fabulous and satisfying or disastrous and terrifying. A relationship can either be so good we make no room for another or so bad we refuse to take a second risk. Our last loss can forfeit our next gain. A nightmare can kill our lifelong dream.

A relationship can either be so good we make no room for another or so bad we refuse to take a second risk.

The word "triangulation" has met us at the door all five days this week. Perhaps seeing it each day has made your skin crawl, because you've experienced the negative side of it. You've encountered triads of people in which one person is detrimental to the relationship between the other two. So have I. It's enough to unsettle any of us. Connectedness has too important a place in Christian theology for the enemy not to attempt to counterfeit it with disastrous triangulations. If he can't ensnare us then he'll try to scare us. When the pen is in the hand of God, however, and He's the one connecting the dots and drawing triangles, mutual joys abound, missing pieces are found, and a network emerges for the sake of the gospel.

Of course, that doesn't mean it's all fun and games. Adjustments often need to be made and some of them are painful. Take Timothy, for instance.

> **REREAD ACTS 16:1-5.** What was the first thing Paul insisted he do and why?

Many students and scholars of Paul's letters through the centuries have found his insistence on Timothy's circumcision intriguing if not baffling. After all, he profusely opposed believers in Christ being forced under the yoke of the Old Testament law.

TAKE THE TIME TO READ ALL 21 VERSES OF GALATIANS 2, AND THEN COMPLETE THE FOLLOWING:

Who had also accompanied Paul according to Galatians 2:3?

Give Titus 1:4 a quick glance. How did Paul describe him?

Yet, how did his inclusion with Paul recorded in Galatians 2:3 differ from Timothy's?

Carefully compare Galatians 2:3 and Acts 16:1. Record any other technical differences between the two young men.

Why did Paul confront Cephas (another name for the apostle Peter) (Gal. 2:11-13)?

How can you know for certain this conflict preceded Timothy accompanying Paul? (Hint: Gal. 2:13)

On Day Four you read God's command to Abraham regarding circumcision in Genesis 17:9-14.

When were boys supposed to be circumcised (Gen. 17:12)?

Timothy was a long way from infancy in Acts 16:3. Why do you suppose he hadn't been circumcised (Acts 16:1,3)?

Timothy's precise age when Paul circumcised him is unknown but we can hover over the neighborhood based on a few indications. Our series is based on Paul's second letter to Timothy but we will often cross-reference the first letter he wrote him.

Q & A

Ruth: *I'm wondering, have you gone through seasons in ministry where you felt devalued and opposed and it seemed easier to quit and save yourself the conflict?*

Beth: *Can you turn up the volume really loud for this answer please? YES! Sometimes God used those things to prepare me for a move or a major transition, almost as if He were weaning me off my attachment to an environment that had served its purpose in my life. He never fails to put insult, conflict, and opposition to some kind of use. Sometimes He uses them to show me I'm in the wrong or to simply test my perseverance, humble me, and starve my approval addiction. The reason I haven't quit serving in 30 years truly has nothing to do with me and everything to do with Jesus. In all the ups and downs, tears and fears, conflicts and disappointments, Jesus was still infinitely better than the circumstances were hard. He was just worthy of hanging in there for.*

What indication did Paul give about Timothy's age in 1 Timothy 4:12?

"Young" gets younger and younger as our postmodern culture grows more and more youth-obsessed. To the ancients, however, the term applied all the way up to the age of forty. See there? In the course of one sentence of Bible study, some of you just hopped in a time machine and, voilà, you were young again. According to Irenaeus, one of the early church fathers, "The first stage of life embraces thirty years, and that this extends onwards to the fortieth year, everyone will admit."[19] At the time Paul wrote the first letter to Timothy, referring to him as "young," Timothy was serving as leader of the church in Ephesus.

> *Luke called Paul a "young man" (Acts 7:58) when he was of the same age range as Timothy [in 1 Timothy 4:12]. Timothy's age, in his thirties (the estimate most would agree on), might seem to be a handicap in the Ephesian community, where some of the other believers and other elders are older.[20]*

Okay, let's do the math. First Timothy was written between A.D. 62 and 64. Scholars estimate that Timothy joined Paul approximately A.D. 49 (Acts 16:1). If Timothy was in his thirties when 1 Timothy was written in 62-64, subtract about 13 years and you have a young man hovering somewhere around 20 years old when he joined Paul. Don't go swearing by it though. He could have been as young as fifteen. Jewish boys entered manhood with adolescence and Timothy's parents could conceivably have sent him off with a hug and a sack lunch by that time. Here's a firm grasp of the obvious: the man considered "young" in 1 Timothy 4:12 was very young in Acts 16:1. In all the subtraction, don't miss the fine impression. As young as he was, "the brothers in Lystra and Iconium" already "spoke highly of him" (Acts 16:2). By late adolescence, that young half-breed's godly reputation left footprints all over Lystra then marched all the way to Iconium.

We'd be tempted to say Timothy hit the ground running on his missionary journey if not for that circumcision. Chances are, he limped a little, a gait similar to his forefather Jacob who got to embrace his new God-given identity with his hip popped out of socket (Gen. 32:25-28). Many of us have walked onto the path of our divine calling with a wounding. Perhaps it's time we quit thinking that it's accidental.

Imagine Titus hearing about Timothy's induction into ministry. Don't you know he was immediately relieved to be full-blood Greek? You see, this was the line in the sand drawn by the flint knife of Paul: Timothy was considered a Jew because his mother was Jewish. If he were uncircumcised, he'd pose a stumbling block to virtually every Jew he and Paul would encounter for the

Many of us have walked onto the path of our divine calling with a wounding. Perhaps it's time we quit thinking that it's accidental.

sake of the gospel. The Jerusalem Conference recorded in Acts 15 had already landed a decision regarding Gentile converts:

> Gentiles would not be required to become Jews in order to be Christians. The converse was also true: Jews would not be required to abandon their Jewishness in order to become Christians. There is absolutely no evidence that Paul ever asked Jews to abandon circumcision as their mark of membership in God's covenant people … Paul always worked through the Jewish synagogues where possible. To have had a member of his entourage be of Jewish lineage and yet uncircumcised would have hampered his effectiveness among the Jews. It was at the very least a matter of missionary strategy to circumcise Timothy (1 Cor 9:20). It may have been much more. Paul never abandoned his own Jewish heritage. He may well have wanted Timothy to be true to his (cf. Rom 3:1f.).[21]

Good job this week, student of Scripture. I hope the journeys of Paul and Timothy are causing you to think about yours. After all, you've been called to a missionary journey of your own. During our five weeks together, we will work on documenting ours through parallels to Paul and Timothy's.

Our first step involves the keys below. They represent key people who have been used by God to unlock something that turned out to be crucial on the path of your divine calling. You may be too new to the faith to list as many as five, so please feel no pressure to do so. Just list the ones who have intersected your journey so far.

Write each name beside a key. What did God unlock in you through each key person? Share in the space provided.

I'll see you in the Session Two video!

You've been called to a missionary journey of your own.

13 yrs into their relationship when 2 Tim was written (Timothy is in early 30's)

Phylacteries — worn on forehead

Group Session Two

WATCH THE VIDEO—PURPOSE AND GRACE

INTRODUCTION

Today's session will offer us a glimpse of Paul's first letter to Timothy. It will also officially establish the concept captured in the title of our six-week study.

Three books of the New Testament comprise what is commonly termed the
~~The~~ Pastoral ~~Pastoral~~ Epistles: ~~Epistles~~ 1 Tim,
2 Tim , and Titus . (PE)

PE   Pastoral Epistles

The personal application for our entire six-week course can be summed up in one exhortation:

> O Timothy, guard the deposit entrusted to you.
> **1 TIMOTHY 6:20, ESV**

1 Tim 1:11
God is asking are we trustworthy?

Ramona ~~you~~ guard the Gospel that you have been entrusted with. I am counting on you Ramona.

1. We won't _Effectively_ guard _____ what
we _don't_ _highly_ _esteem_ .

"The combination of verb and noun 'guard the deposit' ... was used in the ancient world of the high obligation of having in trust _Another_ _persons_ _treasured_ _possession_ , of keeping it _safe_ , and of returning it _as_ _it_ _was_ ."
Dr. G.W. Knight[1]

2. If we ___Cant___ ___stand___ to ___be___ ___questions___, we will be ___too___ ___childish___ to ___stand___ ___guard___.

Anyone beyond question is also maybe beyond ___character___.

Laws of Applause from Andy Stanley[2]
- What's applauded as exceptional the first time will be ___expected___ the next time.

- Those most applauded for feel most ___entitled___ to. (dangerous)

- Applause is ___addictive___. (scary)

3. The sign of a great potential leader ___is___ ___NOT___ the ___eagerness___ to ___take___ ___charge___. It's the eagerness ___to___ ___take___ ___the___ ___change___.

The trust is the Gospel of the Lord Jesus Christ.

1. George W. Knight, III, *The Pastoral Epistles, New International Greek Testament Commentary* (Grand Rapids, MI: Wm. B. Eerdmans Publishing Co., 1992), 276.
2. Andy Stanley, as quoted by Jenni Catron, "Catalyst 2013," *JenniCatron.com* (Online) 3 October 2013 [cited 7 July 2016]. Available from the Internet: JenniCatron.com.

Purpose and Grace

Day One

A CLEAR CONSCIENCE

FLASH FORWARD: *I thank God, whom I serve with a clear conscience.*
2 TIMOTHY 1:3A

What happens when a man who has lived the equivalent, roughly speaking, of nine average lives, traveled some ten thousand miles on foot, boat, or beast, had enough comrades to populate a small town, and has seen jaw-dropping wonders suddenly gets chained down and left almost entirely alone?

What happens ...

... when a man once blinded by the blazing glory of the risen Christ is at the mercy of whatever light can filter through a crude hole?

... when a man who has spread the fragrance of Christ shares a breezeless space with human waste?

... when a man who has cheated death again and again lifts his chin to face its imminence?

... when a man who'd glimpsed the highest heaven is shut up in an underground pit?

Before we answer for him, let's turn the tables and imagine ourselves as well-traveled, people-immersed, bigger-than-life survivors shackled to a dungeon floor anticipating the blade of a killer sword. Because we are people of faith wrapped in human flesh, our responses would most likely bounce off the walls in various extremes depending on the hour.

How do you imagine you'd pass the hours at your worst and then at your best?

AT YOUR WORST ...	AT YOUR BEST ...
Crying begging screaming	praying Praising singing

Beth: *God is astonishingly faithful. What He wills, He works. Keith and I don't serve in ministry side-by-side but his support, prayer, and counsel are imperative to me. In some ways the fact that he hasn't shared my occupation has worked to our advantage. We've gotten to have a family life that hasn't been totally invaded by ministry.*

Some of us might lose our minds before we lost our heads. To our inestimable benefit, Paul hung onto his. His responses have continued to bear light, hope, counsel, courage, and consolation for centuries.

PLEASE READ 2 TIMOTHY 1:1-3 AND, IF YOU'RE PARTICIPATING IN THIS LEVEL OF THE EXPERIENCE, PLEASE HANDWRITE THAT PASSAGE IN THE BACK OF THE BOOK (PAGE 180). Two of Paul's responses glare at you wide-eyed in the third verse.

Fill in the following blanks according to any major translation:
I thank God, whom I serve with a clear conscience as my ancestors did, when I constantly __Remember__ you in my __prayers__ night and day.

He remembered. He prayed. These responses will spring to life in the journey we have ahead, but both would be lost to us if Paul hadn't had a third response: he *wrote*. And not just to anyone. To someone he loved like his own skin.

What term of endearment does Paul give Timothy in verse 2?

my dear son

COMPARE 2 TIMOTHY 1:2 TO 1 TIMOTHY 1:2. Do you sense any intensification in the second letter? If so, in what way?

Yes Timothy went from a son in the faith to my dear son

We owe a debt of gratitude to God that Paul's words were not just inspired by love and limited to one. They were inspired by the Holy Spirit and extended to all. Today we've unfolded the letter we will dog-ear for the next four weeks. The fettered prisoner is almost certainly "writing" the letter through oral dictation, perhaps to Luke since Paul mentions later in the letter that Luke alone is with him (4:11). With every verse you read throughout our study, imagine it coming from the voice of one personally involved, completely invested, and thoroughly convinced that much was at stake.

Paul, an apostle of Christ Jesus *dia thelematos theou*: "through the will of God."
2 TIMOTHY 1:1

If your head was about to roll because of crimes against the emperor, being utterly certain you'd been called by no one less than God and acted in nothing less than His will could be the difference between sanity and madness and between acceptance and abject terror. Paul opened nine of his thirteen letters with similar qualifiers, pounding the point like a carpenter pounds a nail. He had not called himself. Indeed Paul *would not* have called himself. He saw himself not only as "the least of the apostles, unworthy to be called an apostle" (1 Cor. 15:9) but "the least of all the saints" (Eph. 3:8), *saints* being a term he employed for all who were in Christ.

BUT HERE'S THE GORGEOUS JUXTAPOSITION. How did Paul serve according to 2 Timothy 1:3?

He serves as his ancestors did w/ a clear conscience.

Behold a rare gem: a person with a crystal clean conscience who takes zero credit. If we could reach the conclusion of this study utterly convinced we have a divine calling and equally convinced we did nothing to earn it, not one moment of this journey will be wasted. Those two convictions would supply both the confidence and humility we desperately need to be powerfully and miraculously used by God. Paul's reference to serving God with a clear conscience in the immediate context of the phrase *as my ancestors did* emphasizes the unapologetic continuity he saw between his present faith in Christ and the faith of his ancestors. Paul didn't specify or explain what ancestors he was referring to. It's probable that he meant the patriarchs, prophets, and other Old Testament saints, but he could also have been referring to other believers in the early church.[1]

In its broader context as a man's final testament of his life, a conscience that was clear spoke volumes of a God who was good. After all, this clear conscience was embedded in the heart of ...

> ... one who was formerly a blasphemer, a persecutor, and an arrogant man. But I received mercy because I acted out of ignorance in unbelief. And the grace of our Lord overflowed, along with the faith and love that are in Christ Jesus. This saying is trustworthy and deserving of full acceptance: "Christ Jesus came into the world to save sinners"—and I am the worst of them.
>
> 1 TIMOTHY 1:13-15

> If we could reach the conclusion of this study utterly convinced we have a divine calling and equally convinced we did nothing to earn it, not one moment of this journey will be wasted.

Again I see we are called to be here at this table — we are called to serve not because of us. divinely — Know it.

PAUL HAD BEEN THE BELIEVING RECIPIENT OF A WORK DESCRIBED IN HEBREWS 10:19-23. Read this passage and record the basis of "a true heart in full assurance of faith."

when we come to Christ w/ a right attitude, not out of obligation but rather out of desire — we have a true heart — Jesus makes a way for us — faith in Jesus to be family w/ God

I want to share something I learned the hard way. If you don't let God deal with your guilty conscience, you'll lack assurance, hemorrhage faith, and default to so much condemnation, you'll cripple your walk with Christ. A miserably heavy conscience can result from a wide range of wrong-doing:

betraying someone, devastating someone, breaking somebody's heart, getting someone fired, telling something we shouldn't have, deceiving someone, livingly duplicitously and carrying on a secret life, being grossly selfish to the detriment of others, heaping the same thing on our loved ones that got heaped on us. We can even genuinely repent and turn our backs on the sin and seek forgiveness from people we hurt and still carry the terrible burden of guilt for years on end.

That happens to me all the time. But how do I stop it?

Until we let Christ's work on the cross not only save our souls but cleanse our consciences, our own self-destructive tendencies will unwittingly team with the devil to bully us with bouts of mental torment. You may reason as I reasoned for years: *well, at least it keeps me humble.* But, unfortunately, that's not all a guilty conscience does. It also sets you up for self-sabotage. You'll be on the way to something good and do something ridiculous. You will have an overwhelming tendency to repeat the same pattern you've despised in yourself because, somewhere deep inside, you still believe the old you is the real you.

A guilty conscience can't keep its mouth shut. It constantly recounts your regrets and reminds you of what you deserve, drowning out the liberating voice of truth. Until the matter gets settled at the foot of the cross and you realize your heart has been sprinkled clean with the blood of Christ, the joy of every victory in Christ will be hijacked in record time by a baffling self-disdain.

> A guilty conscience can't keep its mouth shut.

Is any part of this discussion resonating with you personally? If so, explain how.

Yes - Can't let go of old ugly things I have done -

Those who never lay down a long-burdened conscience tend to respond to the suggestion of true freedom from guilt with this rebuttal under their breath: "You have no idea what I've done." Jesus might wish to counter with this: "Actually, you have no idea what *I've* done." To grasp the gloriously good news of Hebrews 10:19-23, let's trace the history of the word pictures.

FIRST, READ HEBREWS 9:11-22. This segment contrasts and compares the first covenant (also called the Old Covenant) with the New Covenant.

What essential difference does it describe between the two?

Blood of animals vs the blood of Jesus

What essential similarity does it describe between the two?

Blood to clean + sanctify

entrusted

The original scene described in Hebrews 9:18-20 is found in
Exodus 24:1-11 so let's give it a look. What did the people assure
Moses they would do in Exodus 24:3?

They said they would do what God said

What did Moses then do in Exodus 24:8?

Covered or sprinkled blood on the people as a sign of this covenant

What astonishing scene is depicted in Exodus 24:9-11?

People ~~talking with~~ seeing God - God on a pavement of beautiful blue -

With this background still in view, flip back to Hebrews 10:19-23. Focus on
verse 22.

> Let us draw near with a true heart in full assurance of
> faith, our hearts sprinkled clean from an evil conscience
> and our bodies washed in pure water.
> HEBREWS 10:22

Circle the words *sprinkled* and *washed.*

The agent of the washing is water and the agent of the sprinkling is blood.
Do you want to see something fascinating? Glance at Exodus 29. The
chapter describes the intricate process of consecrating the priests who
would serve in the tabernacle under the first covenant.

To make the connection with Hebrews 10:22, you need only read two
verses. Record the act of consecration taken in each:
EXODUS 29:4

Wash w/ water (baptism?)

EXODUS 29:21

Sprinkled w/ blood + oil to consecrate

Consecrate means having been made or declared sacred / setting yourself aside set apart

Nothing exhilarates me more than watching Scripture connect the dots. Beholding the brilliance of the Word is a holy high to me. I hope it lights up your soul, too. Let's bring home the point with one more connection. This side of Christ's death, resurrection, and the birth of His church, the priesthood is not limited to a select few among God's people. It is comprised of every Jesus follower. First Peter 2 calls us a "holy priesthood" (v. 5) and a "royal priesthood" (v. 9). Revelation 1:5-6 heralds the process with this praise.

> To Him who loves us and has set us free from our sins by His blood, and made us a kingdom, priests to His God and Father— the glory and dominion are His forever and ever. Amen.
> **REVELATION 1:5-6**

> By His blood. By that same sacrifice, our hearts have been sprinkled clean from an evil conscience.
> **HEBREWS 10:22**

On the cross, Jesus took what we deserved. He gave His life not only as our sin offering but our guilt offering. He paid an inconceivably high price to bear our guilt upon the cross. Our insistence on carrying it long after genuine repentance is an act of unbelief. In the words of 2 Corinthians 5:21, "He made the One who did not know sin to be sin for us, so that we might become the righteousness of God in Him."

He gave His life not only as our sin offering but our guilt offering.

If you struggle to truly believe this exchange, whisper the words of the desperate man in Mark 9:24, "Help my unbelief." This is the power of the cross. This is the enormity of God's love. A guilty conscience does not guarantee humility. It guarantees misery. It does not guard you from falling back into the same pattern. It taunts you back. Confess your sins if you haven't already and repent with a change of mind. Then, child of God, receive what Jesus has already accomplished for you. Our humility comes from never forgetting Jesus took our place and that all we are called to be and to do is a gift of grace. Your back is tired, Beloved. Lay down the heavy burden of your guilty conscience. Jesus has sprinkled your heart clean.

This was very confusing ?? Do I sound like this??

Timothy, the Corinthians, AND Paul's Way of Life in Christ

We're going a little heavy on the theological ideas this week but be of good cheer, the concepts we are working with have the potential to make us better Bible readers. We have no time to waste, so let's jump right in!

In 1 Corinthians, one of my favorite letters in the New Testament, the apostle Paul includes an intriguing note that we would probably miss if we weren't keeping an eye out for Timothy. At the apex of an elaborate argument regarding his apostleship, Paul informs the Corinthian church that he has sent Timothy to Corinth to remind them of his way of life in Christ (1 Cor. 4:16-17). Timothy must have been expected in Corinth shortly after the Corinthians received Paul's letter. Take a few seconds to read 1 Corinthians 4:14-17 for yourself:

> "I am writing this not to shame you but to warn you as my dear children. Even if you had ten thousand guardians in Christ, you do not have many fathers, for in Christ Jesus I became your father through the gospel. Therefore I urge you to imitate me. For this reason I have sent you Timothy, my son whom I love, who is faithful in the Lord. He will remind you of my way of life in Christ Jesus, which agrees with what I teach everywhere in every church" (NIV).

The Corinthians had not matured at the pace Paul expected, but were still spiritual infants (3:1), not able to digest anything but milk (3:2). Quarrels and divisions ran rampant as some were claiming one Christian leader over against and above another. As the letter unfolds Paul faults the Corinthians, or at least a group of them, with some kind of over-realized eschatology.

Let's stop right there. What in the real world where people actually live is "over-realized" eschatology? Before we get around to answering that question, let's define two concepts: 1) realized eschatology and 2) future eschatology. These are terms theology nerds like myself use at dinner parties. If "eschatology" in general is the study of the final things, then "realized eschatology" is the teaching that the final things have already happened, and "future eschatology" is the teaching that the final things are yet to come.[1] Both concepts are taught in and across the New Testament, and so both ideas must be maintained in some way. Fred Sanders said it well: "Realized eschatology has to be kept in constant, creative tension with future eschatology."[2] Problems arise, however, when one of them is emphasized at the expense of the other or the two are not understood together.

Eschatology = Prophecy

This brings us back to our most important term today: *over-realized eschatology*. Bear with me. If "realized eschatology" is the teaching that the final things have already happened, an "over-realized eschatology" is a theology that misunderstands or exaggerates the extent to which the final things have already occurred and thus have affected the believer's current experience.[3] (Disclaimer: To keep things as simple as possible here I am making a distinction between realized eschatology and over-realized eschatology. But in some theological circles these terms may be used and understood differently or even interchangeably.) While it is true we have supernatural power and authority in Christ, an over-realized eschatology tends to emphasize these things to such an exaggerated extent that it fails to give adequate weight to experiences of suffering, weakness, and lack in the Christian experience. Although it rightly elevates the resurrection of Christ, an over-realized eschatology wrongly diminishes a theology of the cross of Christ, despite the reality of a world so devastatingly full of death and suffering. An over-realized eschatology is a theology that is too triumphant.

Let's do a little Christian theology review. In simplest theological terms, there are two ages: "this age" and "the age to come."[4] The former lasts from creation to the return of Christ while the latter refers to the age when God's everlasting reign will be consummated.[5] Paul describes Christians as those upon whom "the end of the ages has come" (1 Cor. 10:11, ESV) and while they have received the Holy Spirit and hence also many spectacular gifts, they have not yet begun to fully reign with Christ in glory. But even though the kingdom has not yet been fully consummated since Christ has not returned, because of His life, death, and resurrection believers experience aspects of "the age to come" even in "this age." Michael Horton does a brilliant job summarizing how the Bible articulates this paradoxical reality. "Biblical scholars call this liminal space in between these two ages the 'already-not yet.'"[6]

"Scripture assures believers that they have already passed from death to life, that they have already 'put on Christ' in baptism and have been raised with him in newness, seated with him in the heavenlies. They were enemies, but now they are God's friends and children. They were in bondage to sin and guilt, but now they are liberated to serve God and are justified freely by God's grace. That future verdict of the day of judgment is announced already here and now, as believers are already declared righteous. Furthermore, they were characterized by unrighteousness according to the image of fallen Adam but are now being conformed to the image of Christ. This is the rescripting that has made believers definitively new. At the same time, they continue to sin and find unbelief, hypocrisy, and self-righteousness even in their noblest thoughts and deeds. In other words, they live in the wilderness, between the exodus and the Promised Land, redeemed but not redeemed, saved but not saved, liberated but not liberated. And despite the fact that their blindness has been healed they still 'see in a mirror, dimly, but then face to face' (1 Cor. 13:12, NKJV)."[7]

A tension emerges from Scripture itself that is crucial to understanding the Christian life. As Horton puts it, "Believers never live in either the already or the not yet by itself but always in that in-between world, moving back and forth between these two realities."[8] Christian theology is full of already-not yet tension.

Wow, that was a ridiculous amount of theological jargon for a two-page lesson, right? Thank you for hanging in there with me! Ponder these ideas on your own time. In the next article we will explore them further, noting how they apply to Paul, Timothy, and the Corinthian situation. I think these matters also have no small amount of relevance for us today.

Day Two

I REMEMBER

FLASH FORWARD: *... clearly recalling your sincere faith that first lived in your grandmother Lois, then in your mother Eunice, and that I am convinced is in you also.* **2 TIMOTHY 1:5**

We launched the second week with a series of questions I'll sum up with one: What does a person like Paul do when he's lived so much life and labored with so many people then faces his life's violent end almost alone? We began scripting an answer with three verbs: He *remembered*. He *prayed*. He *wrote*. We'll reach back to that lesson, grab the word "remembered" and drag it into this one.

PLEASE READ 2 TIMOTHY 1:4-7 AND WRITE IT IN THE BACK OF YOUR BOOK (PAGE 180). We will focus on verses 4 and 5 today, sequestering verses 6 and 7 for the video teaching in Session Three.

> Remembering your tears, I long to see you
> so that I may be filled with joy.
> **2 TIMOTHY 1:4**

Paul feels Timothy to not be timid - I picture a boy raised by 2 women w/ a father not there a lot - he is timid -

Here a distinction floats to the surface, setting the Paul/Timothy paradigm slightly apart from teacher/student or mentor/mentee paradigms. All three paradigms are profoundly important and can be equally impactful, but 2 Timothy 1:4 attaches an intensifier to the first one: *vulnerable love*. While endearment can be elemental in all three relationships, the Paul/Timothy paradigm cannot exist apart from it or qualify without it. Their paradigm requires a more vulnerable love. I'll try to demonstrate the difference. By God's astonishing grace, I continually get to be involved in the teacher/student relationship from both sides. Every time I open a commentary or listen to a podcast, I take the side of student. As I write these sentences, I cartwheel to the other side and become teacher. I became startlingly aware in my early 30s just how much God meant what He said in 1 Corinthians 13:1-3.

Sum up the segment in your own words.

If we work - give - struggle to gain God's pleasure - we are falling backwards into faith thru works - we fail - when we do these things with the right heart - out of love and as acts of worship to God - then we do them right - Grace - not works lest anyone should boast

I could blacken my lungs burning midnight oil studying the Scriptures and lose my eyesight to endless footnotes in commentaries but if I did not love the groups I taught, every moment of the lesson would rise to God's ears like an incessant nerve-grating gong. What a disturbing thought. If God didn't like what He heard in my classes, who cared if anyone else did? I started actively praying for God to give me a supernatural love for the people I teach. Bless His name, He did. Many years later and as recently as last night, I still get tears in my eyes over a note from, an encounter with, or sometimes just a picture of someone I've gotten to serve. I've also had the privilege to mentor a smaller number of women, forming relationships that are so deeply satisfying and dear to me. I can genuinely claim love as an active agent in both kinds of relationships in my life. Still, the Paul/Timothy dynamic pushes participants further than that. It shoves you out there where your heart is exposed to the elements, to a place where you can really get hurt.

I woke up thinking about these deep relationships this morning and jotted down the following words without making an iota of connection to this lesson:

The raw vulnerability of untempered love. Of that handful of people who hold your heart—skinned alive—and could slay you with their absence. Untempered love is terrifying. But what's life if we never love others past the rational sensibilities of our self-protection?

> What's life if we never love others past the rational sensibilities of our self-protection?

I'd awakened thinking about the family cookout we'd had two nights earlier. My dearest loves in all the world were there. Each one of them holds my heart skinned-alive in his or her hands, even the tiny one with a palm the size of a pecan. The word "slay" may be a little melodramatic for some. What I mean is our raw vulnerability to people whose absence could, figuratively speaking, *nearly kill us.* If you're fairly emotive, the absence doesn't have to be permanent. When my firstborn, Amanda, moved to northern England with her newlywed husband for five months of ministry, she didn't let me drive them to the airport. "Dad is going to take us, Mom," she announced with just enough mist in her eyes for me to reason why. As much as he loved her, they were less likely to make a scene than a girl and her mother.

As we'll soon demonstrate, vulnerable love is by no means limited to family. In fact, sometimes our family dynamics are so complicated and cold, we need to wear a bomber jacket to supper.

With these distinctions in mind, name some people who hold your *heart skinned* alive in their hands:

Mike
Bob
Suzy
Mom
Bill

entrusted

The Paul/Timothy paradigm is in some ways even more impressive than the traditional parent/child paradigm. Can you think of any reasons why?

I'll throw one out there: because it's voluntary. It's chosen *by* you rather than *for* you. You didn't choose your parents. And, even if your parents chose you, unless you were already mostly grown, they didn't really know whom they were choosing. The vulnerability of heart within the traditional family context is primarily compulsory. It goes with the territory and it's a beautiful thing. Something has gone awry when it is absent.

Paul, on the other hand, was a single man with no children. He could have kept a wider emotional distance and no one would have been the wiser. Instead, he opened himself up to *Timothy, my dearly loved son.* Think of a small handful of people so dear to you, you'd call for them from your deathbed. That was Timothy to Paul. Vulnerable love doesn't just hope to see. It *longs.* Paul didn't have the luxury of only recalling Timothy's laugh. He also remembered Timothy's *tears.* You see, we treasure memories of laughter from many we gave little access to our hearts. Perhaps we really liked them. But Paul and Timothy's relationship went far beyond the happy-go-lucky safety of *like.* Evidently the younger cried right in front of him and the older couldn't shake the memory from his mind. "Come quickly!" Paul seemed to say. "Replace this sorrowful picture pinned on the wall of my mind with a face stretched wide with joy!"

mom-dad-bill- my kids
friends -

Vulnerable love
doesn't just hope
to see. It longs.

Paul may have seen Timothy's tears countless times but several scholars wonder if the scene he couldn't shake was recorded in Acts 20. We can only theorize because we won't find this *dearly loved son* mentioned by name in those verses but the poignancy tenderly displays the deep bond between Paul and those he'd trained to serve. Let's do a little background even if some segments are familiar to you from our opening session.

READ 1 TIMOTHY 1:3. Where had Timothy been assigned and why?

Ephesus to stop false teaching

Where did Paul say he was going when he urged Timothy to remain behind?

Macedonia

To determine where Paul served in Acts 19, glance at the paragraph headings, or quickly peruse the chapter. List the locations.

Ephesus, Macedonia, Achaia, Jerusalem,

What did Paul do in Acts 20:1?

Set out for Macedonia

This may be the point at which Paul first left Timothy behind as his apostolic representative to guard and grow the young church in Ephesus. Timothy's stay at this point could only have been temporary, however, because his name is recorded among those once again with Paul several months later (Acts 20:4). Now, let's proceed toward a scene of tears to wonder if Timothy's were among them. According to Acts 20:15, Paul and his companions docked in Miletus, the port just south of Ephesus. From there Paul summoned the Ephesian elders to come meet with him (Acts 20:17).

READ ACTS 20:16-38. How long had Paul served in Ephesus? *3 year*

Describe the scene in Acts 20:36-38.

a group of men saying farewell (probably for the last time to someone that they became Christians thru — Line saying goodbye to frieda — ouch.

Divine love does not spare itself.

Welcome to the heart-skinning of soul closeness. This is what happens when you don't just offer your gifts. You offer your heart and it can get torn right out of your chest. Still, we keep putting it out there because what is love without sacrifice in the wake of Christ's cross? A life that risks no loss is no life at all. Divine love does not spare itself. If Timothy was witness to that emotional farewell or perhaps entrusted to the elders at that time, as tender as Paul would have been to them all, the tears of one stung most of all. "I remember your tears," he wrote close to his death (2 Tim. 1:4, ESV).

WIDEN THE SCOPE FROM 2 TIMOTHY 1:4 TO THE VERSES BOOKENDING IT. Notice the linked theme of heritage in both verse 3 and verse 5. Check the context of these verses and offer your thoughts on why Paul may have made a point of bringing up spiritual lineage. *Maybe to strengthen his desire to be a father to Timothy — he talks about his ancestors & then Timothy's mother & grandmother —*

Profound thoughts about ancestry didn't originate with humans. God unfolded the concept as early as Genesis then incorporated it into His self-disclosure to Moses in Exodus 3:6: "I am the God of your father, the God of Abraham, the God of Isaac, and the God of Jacob."

Practically every child of God has an earthly spiritual ancestry. Imagine in the eternal realm if, without explanation, God ordered us all in multiple strands of immensely long lines fanning outward from one starting point. Imagine if He, then, through thundering voice, said, "Behold your lineage of faith." Talk about the ultimate meet and greet. If I could script the scene, He'd also lift Abraham to the highest rung of a ladder to absorb the sight since his stunning act of obedience in Genesis 22 welcomed God to make and keep this promise: "I will indeed bless you and make your offspring as numerous as the stars of the sky and the sand on the seashore" (v. 17).

Taking personal ownership of our spiritual lineage—both in what we receive and what we pass down—is titanic in this Scriptural journey. Whether we are on the younger side of the generational spectrum or older, God's sovereign way is for optimum fruitfulness and faithfulness to spring from the soil of our connectedness.

Spend the next few days thinking about your own spiritual lineage for a diagram we'll fill out down the road. If you're like me, you're not an exact copy of any of your prominent teachers, mentors, or spiritual fathers and mothers. You're a creative blend of all your main influencers mixed in with your own God-given uniqueness.

Think about your spiritual traits and tastes: who you are, what makes you *you*, how you relate with Christ and other people. The ultimate objective of our self-examination is not to add further weight to our gluttonous Me-focus. If we're victorious, it will shift weight to our Them-focus. We will acknowledge what, by God's grace, we have received, what we can steward, and what we can pay forward "so that a future generation—children yet to be born—might know. They were to rise and tell their children so that they might put their confidence in God and not forget God's works, but keep His commands" (Ps. 78:6-7).

The reports of Jesus revealing Himself in dreams to some people in countries shut tight to the gospel tempers my dogmatism here.

You're a creative blend of all your main influencers mixed in with your own God-given uniqueness.

Day Three

HIS OWN

FLASH FORWARD: *He has saved us and called us with a holy calling, not according to our works, but according to His own purpose and grace, which was given to us in Christ Jesus before time began.* **2 TIMOTHY 1:9**

You are a fine student.

I open with these words for several reasons:

1. You have prioritized studying in the midst of life at break-neck speed. This is no less true even if this is your first attempt at in-depth Bible study.

2. The Spirit of God is at work in your inner being, making a student of you and flourishing in you as you search the deeper things of God. Note 1 Corinthians 2:10-12 in the margin.

3. Thinking you lack what it takes to be a great student of Scripture will lower your level of participation.

I'm going to ask you to complete assignments you may be tempted to skip based on an old track record as a mediocre student or the belief that you'll never be the type to actually enjoy Bible study. If an objection like "I never was good at this kind of thing" rears up in you, shut it down. Your performance in geometry and geography in high school doesn't get to prophesy over your capacity to flourish as a student of Scripture. How much you stand to enjoy poring over Scripture in your pursuit of God is not one whit dependent upon how much you loved history in high school. Even the fact that you never really got into the last Bible study doesn't mean God can't wildly work through this one. Sometimes it's a matter of timing.

You have a great student in you because the Spirit of Truth resides in you. As you study *and keep studying*, He will bear witness to His Word and prosper your soul in a way no one could adequately describe to you.

PLEASE READ 2 TIMOTHY 1:8-10 AND HANDWRITE IT ON THE APPROPRIATE PAGE.

> Now God has revealed these things to us by the Spirit, for the Spirit searches everything, even the depths of God. For who among men knows the thoughts of a man except the spirit of the man that is in him? In the same way, no one knows the thoughts of God except the Spirit of God. Now we have not received the spirit of the world, but the Spirit who comes from God, so that we may understand what has been freely given to us by God.
>
> 1 CORINTHIANS 2:10-12

2 Tim 1:7 for the spirit God gave us does not make us timid, but gives us power, love + self discipline

So Do not be ashamed of the Testimony about our Lord or of me his prisoner. Rather, join with me in suffering for the gospel, by the power of God. He has saved us, + called us to a holy life - not because of anything we have done but because of his own purpose + grace. This grace was given us in Christ Jesus before the beginning of time. but it has now been revealed thru the appearing of our savior Christ Jesus

Cross reference 2 Timothy 1:8 and Romans 1:16 and record their similarities.

The gospel saves - it has power

> So don't be embarrassed to speak up for our Master or for me, his prisoner.
>
> 2 TIMOTHY 1:8 (MSG)

You can't charge Paul with beating around the bush in his second letter to Timothy. He measured his words and got straight to the point like a man trying to beat the clock. *The Message* brings the first phrase home: "don't be embarrassed." The fact is, sometimes we *are* embarrassed. In Paul and Timothy's era, Christ's crucifixion was so recent that the stigma of dishonor was especially acute. Christ's willingness to bear the humiliation of the cross before the exaltation of the crown flew in the face of Israel's expectation of a warrior-like Messiah and liberating king. Crucifixion was for criminals. Lowlifes. The retelling of Christ's passion over the centuries has lessened the stigma but we are not immune to embarrassment for other reasons.

Maybe the God-man didn't man-up enough for us at times. Sometimes I'm more like James and John in Luke 9:54 than I like to admit, wishing Jesus would bring down the fire on His detractors to give them some healthy respect. Maybe I'm also at times like his half-brothers who asked why He didn't just go ahead and work outrageous miracles to prove Himself to people (John 7:1-5). Still other times I clam up because I fear the exclusive claim of Christ as the only way to God is going to be mocked or hotly challenged in my current environment.

Do any of these examples resonate with you? Explain. *Absolutely. Being a Bible thumper today is frowned upon - so we stay away when we need to be bold -*

Do you have your own examples? If so, share.

Perhaps little about Christ embarrasses us; it's other Christians who make us cringe.

On a scale of 1 to 10, with 1 being "I barely notice how other Christians act," and 10 being "I'm totally mortified by how some other Christians act," how on target is this for you? *8*

If we were sitting across from one another, we'd probably have to laugh to cope with our conviction. Our phobia of looking and sounding like those who embarrass us is a Goliath-size inhibitor to the gospel. From the start Satan capitalized on the Homo sapiens' fear of looking stupid.

who has destroyed death & has brought life + immortality to light thru the gospel.

The first four words of the serpent in Genesis 3 are brilliantly constructed to deconstruct the reasoning of the hearer. "Did God really say ...?" Translation: *How gullible could you be?* See, the enemy doesn't have to tempt us into some heinous sin to render us ineffective. All he has to do is bet high on our low threshold for embarrassment. Dr. I.H. Marshall writes, "Shame is a feeling which leads to action which hides witness."[2]

Rewrite that quote in your own words:

Being ashamed + intimidated ~~stops~~ me testimony - ~~the~~ waters it down — Shame on me!

Return to 2 Timothy 1:8. What did Paul tell Timothy to do *instead* of being ashamed?

Do not be ashamed

Synkakopathēson (only here and in 2:3) ... is compounded of *patheō*, "suffer"; *kakos*, "bad"; and *syn*, "together." So it means "bear evil treatment along with," "take one's share of ill-treatment."[3]

Our English phrase *share in suffering* is a one-word mouthful in the Greek *(Synkakopathēson)*.

Would you like to know something interesting? Paul may indeed have coined that compound word. We followers of Jesus fellowship together, work together, worship together, pray together, study the Scriptures together, and, if you and your fellow sojourners are like me and mine, we often eat together and laugh together. Here Paul drives home the point that we must also be willing to suffer together the evil launched against us for carrying the testimony of Jesus. In all these years of writing Bible studies, I cannot remember ever using the idiom *buck up* but I'm about to. We are all Timothys who are called to buck up, take our share of suffering, and quit being dashed and demoralized over every criticism and attack. We live in a culture where Christianity is plummeting in popularity and where we, instead of Satan, are touted as the enemy. If we're going to be unashamed of the gospel, we are undoubtedly going to suffer for its sake.

> If we're going to be unashamed of the gospel, we are undoubtedly going to suffer for its sake.

Take a fresh look at 2 Timothy 1:9-10. Many scholars suggest the exquisite wording is creed-like or, more pointedly, hymn-like. More theology is packed into those two verses than we can possibly unpack in one lesson but my immense hope is that this Bible study as a whole will expound on them.

Notice two references made to time frames in verses 9-10, one in each verse. In the space below, use a straight edge and draw a time line connecting two bold dots. Leave space above the line and at each end for labeling and documentation.

Grace was given to us before the beginning of time Creation

Christ destroyed death

Jesus appearing Grace was revealed

Label the bold dot at the beginning of the line "Creation" and the one at the end "Christ's appearing."

We can know that time "began" at creation because Genesis 1:1 says "in the beginning God created." There is no beginning or end, no tick-tock of the clock, in the eternal realm. Thus "beginning" is a reference to God's induction of time in regard to the temporal realm.

Now, return to your time line and document to the left of the first bold dot what happened before time began (according to 2 Tim. 1:9-10) and above the second bold dot what was made evident when Christ appeared. In the space to the right of the second bold dot, document what Christ accomplished according to verse 10.

Two thousand years later, salvation still comes exactly the same way Paul and Timothy received it. So, if God saved us and called us "according to His own purpose and grace, which was given to us in Christ Jesus before time began," how much did our works have to do with it? *nothing*

Describe what that fact means to you personally. *A ton! At first I think 'well hey I have always been a good person' then BOOM I remember really horrendous things I have done I realize nothing I could do can fix those—I am ever grateful to be washed clean. Water could not do that I needed divine blood to cleanse me—Jesus, King Jesus*

Appreciate the words "His own" in 2 Timothy 1:9. What two things were God's "own"? __*Purpose*__ *Gods* and __*grace*__ *Gods*.

The Greek word for *purpose* is *prosthesis*. It conveys "a setting forth, presentation, an exposition, determination, plan, or will. It involves purpose, resolve, and design. A placing in view or openly displaying something."[4]

What part of that definition jumps out at you and why?

determination—resolve-design

Something popped out to me in the definition of the Greek word for *purpose* that may mean as much to you as it does to me. The antonym or opposite of *prosthesis* (purpose) is *metánoia*, the Greek term that translates "*repentance, change of mind*."[5] Not only were you saved and called by His own purpose before time began, He hasn't changed His mind for a single moment since.

Bathe in this definition for *cháris*, the basic Greek word for *grace*. Dunk your head in it and splash in it.

> Not only were you saved and called by His own purpose before time began, He hasn't changed His mind for a single moment since.

Grace, particularly that which causes joy, pleasure, gratification, favor, acceptance, for a kindness granted or desired, a benefit, thanks, gratitude. A favor done without expectation of return; the absolutely free expression of the loving kindness of God to men finding its only motive in the bounty and benevolence of the Giver; unearned and unmerited favor. Cháris stands in direct antithesis to érga, works, the two being mutually exclusive. God's grace affects man's sinfulness and not only forgives the repentant sinner, but brings joy and thankfulness to him. It changes the individual to a new creature without destroying his individuality (2 Cor. 5:17; Eph. 2:8,9).[6]

Tell me that's not good news! Admit what a relief it is to know that God wasn't in the worst mood in all eternity about saving and calling sinners like us.

You are staring in the face of Paul's doctrine of grace. He maintains this stand throughout his letters. No matter how many miles he traveled, his position on works never budged an inch. Grace carried the former persecutor from his first encounter with Christ until it cradled him at his death. Let that same inexhaustible grace cradle you.

Day Four

BECAUSE I KNOW THE ONE

FLASH FORWARD: *But I am not ashamed, because I know the One I have believed in and am persuaded that He is able to guard what has been entrusted to me until that day.* 2 TIMOTHY 1:12

I fell in love with the second letter to Timothy over the verses we will study today. The words reach out like fingertips to the extremities of Paul's experience, gather up all the complexities, responsibilities, and mysteries involved, and condense them into a single message in the cupped hands of God. First, a disclaimer is needed in case the segment proves anticlimactic. Reading the print on the page is not the moving part. It's the identification. And if you and I are going to become mighty servants loosed on this globe, it's an identification we will ultimately embrace.

PLEASE READ AND THEN HANDWRITE 2 TIMOTHY 1:11-14.

If you are using an HCSB, NIV, ESV, or NASB, you no doubt caught the word that became the title for our series. It surfaces twice in the segment.

To whom is the word *entrusted* applied in verse 12 and in verse 14?

> verse 12 - God
> verse 14 - me + you

Entrusted and *entrusting*. Those two words sum up the daily—sometimes hourly—life of a servant of Christ like few others. The whole interchange between God and child continually comes back to the issue of trust: trusting ourselves entirely to God— our loves, lacks, longings, and our very lives— again and again. Then proving trustworthy by the power of His Spirit again and again with what He entrusts to us. I so hope you were able to view the Session Two video where we introduced the theme "Entrusted" in Paul's first letter to Timothy. We will reference, explore, and expound upon our working definition of the word *entrusted* throughout our series so let's do a brief recap.

TAKE A LOOK AT 1 TIMOTHY 1:11. With what had Paul been entrusted?

> The Gospel

Handwritten margin note:
2 Tim 1:11-14 And of this gospel I was appointed a herald + an apostle + a teacher. That is why I am suffering as I am. Yet this is no cause for shame, because I know in whom I have believed, and am convinced that he is able to guard what I have entrusted to him until that day.

Keep as the pattern of sound teaching, with faith + love in Christ Jesus. Guard the good deposit that was Entrusted to you - guard it w/ the help of the Holy Spirit who lives in us.

Now, take a look at the first sentence of 1 Timothy 6:20 and record what Paul exhorted his son in the faith to do.

guard the Gospel — Turn away from other things,

Paul and Timothy have run their races and crossed the finish line. Their obedience then can't supplant our obedience now. We, of course, don't equate our positions and contributions with theirs but we do bear the responsibility of faithfulness to our own callings (Eph. 4:1). It's our turn here on this globe. Each generation of Jesus-followers must take the baton and each individual follower within that generation is called to do his or her part.

At the end of the video session, we each personalized 1 Timothy 6:20 for the sake of our series by exchanging Timothy's name for ours. Fill your name in the blank to recapture its force:

o ___*Ramona*___, guard the deposit entrusted to you (ESV).

God has entrusted us with the gospel of Jesus Christ and the Holy Spirit-gifting to share it.

Being faithful to a trust we can't define is woefully difficult so we landed on a definition boiled down to its most basic terms: God has entrusted us with the gospel of Jesus Christ and the Holy Spirit-gifting to share it. The gospel and the gifting.

Circle those two G-words and memorize them.

Virtually all else involved in our faithfulness to God will originate, associate, and perpetuate with them.

To bring the concepts home, consider two parallels between Paul's experience and our own.

1. *We are also appointed.* What was Paul appointed according to 2 Timothy 1:11?

   a herald, an apostle + a teacher

We lay no claim on Paul's positions but let the record show, follower of Jesus, you have very much been appointed to positions of your own.

Fill in each of the blanks below with the word *appointed*.
When the Gentiles heard this, they rejoiced and glorified the message of the Lord, and all who had been ___*appointed*___ to eternal life believed (Acts 13:48).

You did not choose Me, but I chose you. I __appointed__ you
that you should go out and produce fruit and that your fruit should
remain, so that whatever you ask the Father in My name, He will give
you (John 15:16).

From one man He has made every nationality to live over the whole
earth and has determined their __appointed__ times and
the boundaries of where they live (Acts 17:26).

You have been appointed to eternal life. You, like those first Jesus-followers,
have been appointed to go out and produce fruit. In John 15:5, Jesus
specifically stated, "Whoever abides in me and I in him, he it is that bears
much fruit, for apart from me you can do nothing" (ESV).

Circle that word *whoever.*

You are not only called to bear fruit. You are called to bear much fruit. I love
the words of Jesus in John 15:8 and believe they extend with fresh life of the
Spirit to every generation of Jesus-followers: "My Father is glorified by this:
that you produce much fruit and prove to be My disciples."

Those first disciples did their jobs. They cannot do ours. They produced their
own fruit. They cannot produce ours. In Matthew 28:19, Jesus commanded
and commissioned His first followers to "Go, therefore, and make disciples of
all nations." We are among those disciples. We have been appointed by God
to the globe at this juncture in history. "Therefore, we are ambassadors for
Christ, certain that God is appealing through us" (2 Cor. 5:20).

> We have been
> appointed by
> God to the globe
> at this juncture in
> history.

2. *We will also suffer at times because of our appointment.* Fill in
   Paul's opening words in 2 Timothy 1:12: __That is why I__
   __am suffering as I am__ but I am not
   ashamed ...

Suffering is an inescapable part of inhaling oxygen in the atmosphere of this
fallen planet. But, under this point, we're not talking about the suffering that
is common to all humans. Paul's paradigm suggests that servants of Jesus
suffer some things in direct correlation to the positions God called them to fill.
A measure of your pain and hardship really is in connection to your calling.
Some of it is spiritual warfare. Some of it is sociological resistance because
the world hates us as it hated Christ (John 15:18-19). Some of it is ordained

by God for our growth, our humility, our compassion, our obedience, our completion, our faith, and, read this carefully, our future commendation, joy, and fellowship in His glory. If we have a throw-down fit and refuse to partake in the sufferings of Christ, we will miss partaking in the explosive joy of that measure of His glory.

Underline 1 Peter 4:13 in the margin.

We set a titanic goal for this series: to become mighty servants of God loosed on the globe with the gospel. To do so, we need to be educated and equipped, open-eyed to what's in play so we won't be dashed and devastated at every hint of suffering. Take 1 Peter 4:12-16 in the margin personally as if it appeared in your inbox straight from God this morning.

When we run into great difficulty or pain in the journey of our calling, we're prone to either cast blame or jump to the conclusion that we must have done something wrong or landed somewhere wrong in our attempt to discern God's will. But sometimes hardship will come because you got it right. As hard as this is to grasp, sometimes suffering bubbles up from the well of God's immeasurable affection and devotion to us. He is not unfeeling. He is all-knowing. Something down the road depends on our present stretch of pavement. This He promises us: the suffering will be brief and the fruit of it as long as eternity (2 Cor. 4:17).

Until we see Jesus face-to-face, our journeys won't be straight lines nearly as often as they will be a series of loops rolling us forward by circling us back to faith. *Entrusted* and *entrusting*. Will we trust Him with the suffering He's entrusted to us? Will we believe He has purpose? Do we have vision enough to believe He's planning one of the biggest harvests of our lives through the seed of the Word we're sowing through this hard season? Desperation can fertilize our soil and tears can water our seed like no ease could ever hope to. Are we willing to believe that right on the other side of this life is a party of epic proportions where we'll ecstatically rejoice and share in His unfathomable inheritance?

> Something down the road depends on our present stretch of pavement.

Are you presently on a path that has circled you back to faith? If so, how? If not, when was the last time?

always
over + over

REREAD 2 TIMOTHY 1:13. What did Paul tell Timothy to do?

Keep the pattern of his teaching

Salvation by Grace

The HCSB translates the wording, "Hold on to the pattern of sound teaching." Other translations use the phrase *of sound words*. The lexical Greek translated *sound* is *hugiaínō* meaning: "To be healthy, sound, physically well (Eng.: hygiene) ... Metaphorically of persons, to be sound in the faith, meaning firm, pure in respect to Christian doctrine and life (Titus 1:13; 2:2). Of doctrine, meaning sound doctrine, i.e., true, pure, uncorrupted (1 Tim. 1:10; 6:3; 2 Tim. 1:13; 4:3; Titus 1:9; 2:1)."[7]

One Greek scholar translates the phrase, "Hold to the pattern of healthy words."[8]

The adjective *healthy* nearly brings me to tears. God's words have been health to me. God used His words to heal my tormented mind and to piece back together my broken heart. He still uses them every day of my life to bring health to my soul.

> **Does the concept of healthy words speak relevantly to you right now? If so, how?**

What is true individually has even greater ramifications corporately. The church cannot be healthy without holding tightly to God's Word and to sound doctrine. Methods may change but the Bible must remain. And not just opened but pored over. Studied. The Bride of Christ will grow sick and weak without it.

The role of connectedness in our ramped-up effectiveness will be a continuing theme throughout our series. Each generation is meant to train the next but not into its mirror image. Even when Paul instructed the Corinthians to imitate him, he didn't mean they were to take on his personality. Rather, he exhorted them to model his character and godliness, as he modeled Christ. The goal is Christlikeness, not us-likeness. Spiritual daughters are not meant to look and sound just like their spiritual mothers. Neither are spiritual sons to replicate their spiritual fathers. Each generation needs time and space to grow and find its personality and place in the world. But each generation must hold onto the Scriptures for dear life or the Bride of Christ will suffer with poor circulation, heart disease, poor lung capacity, and a dull mind.

This was Paul's unbroken concrete under his feet when life quaked: "I know the One I have believed in and am persuaded that He is able to guard what has been entrusted to me until that day."

Q & A

Marilyn: *At age 54 I was asked by a young lady to be her mentor. I have no idea how to do this and where even to start. Why she picked me I don't know. I feel like I am not worthy of this task. Any advice?*

Beth: *This made me smile because I assure you people don't ask to be mentored by those who have little to offer. She sees something in you she wants. You're mightier than you think. Start by taking her to lunch or coffee and asking what prompted her request. Urge her to be specific. Then, if you have some insight, offer it. In the time frame you have, pick one of her specifics and tell her what has helped you and what you've learned along the way, even the hard way. If God seems to be in it, think about setting another time the next week. Take it one step at a time and perhaps just one question at a time. Established perimeters and boundaries produce thriving mentoring relationships. We don't have to know everything. Just be willing to share anything.*

The Greek verb for *am persuaded* also translates "I am fully convinced."[9] Nothing will substitute for knowing the One you believe in. No one can know Him for you. And no one He knows supplants His knowing you. Faith endures the furious tests by knowing the One in whom it rests.

Thank God we have one another. We were meant to need each other. But nobody is Jesus but Jesus. Every now and then in this perilous journey comes a quickly fleeting moment of perceiving His invisible, inaudible nearness. And that one moment is richer than a month of Sundays in the fellowship of a thousand saints.

> Faith endures the furious tests by knowing the One in whom it rests.

Let No One Despise Him

In an interview with Krista Tippett, the poet Marie Howe said: "All art holds the knowledge that we're both living and dying at the same time. It *can* hold it."[9]

The power is in maintaining the paradox. In a different way but similar spirit, Christians in this age are simultaneously living and dying by the power of God. We spent time in the previous article defining our terms and suggesting that Christian theology at its best holds the "already-not yet" in tension. We are people of the future with both feet on the ground; we are other-worldly and this-worldly. But we mere mortals don't do well living with tension. Instead, we reduce complex realities and drift toward one pole or the other. In the last article we introduced our primary term "over-realized eschatology." But of course the other extreme, "under-realized eschatology," also exists. Christians "who emphasize the already to the detriment of the not yet represent an 'over-realized eschatology', while those who downplay the already in favor of the dominance of the not yet represent an 'under-realized eschatology.'"[10] Both extremes have their problems.

While "under-realized eschatology" is not as relevant to our discussion about the Corinthians, a lot of us err on this side of the spectrum. I am one of them. "Under-realized eschatology is as equally obnoxious and incorrect as the other pole. It is characterized by a defeatist and pessimistic attitude, refusing to acknowledge the ways in which we are presently victorious and experiencing "the age to come." An under-realized person like me needs some realized eschatology in her life. But let's get back to the Corinthians.

With the previous discussion in mind, watch Paul brilliantly point out the "over-realized" eschatology in the Corinthian context.

"Already you have all you want! Already you have become rich! Without us you have become kings! And would that you did reign, so that we might share the rule with you! For I think that God has exhibited us apostles as last of all, like men sentenced to death, because we have become a spectacle to the world, to angels, and to men. We are fools for Christ's sake, but you are wise in Christ. We are weak, but you are strong. You are held in honor, but we in disrepute. To the present hour we hunger and thirst, we are poorly dressed and buffeted and homeless, and we labor, working with our own hands. When reviled, we bless; when persecuted, we endure; when slandered, we entreat. We have become, and are still, like the scum of the world, the refuse of all things."
1 Corinthians 4:8-13, ESV

Those lines, woven with such contrast and irony, are terrific, aren't they? Gordon Fee, one of the foremost commentators on 1 Corinthians, breaks down the sharp disagreement between Paul and the Corinthians like this: "Paul's perspective, which he shares with the rest of the NT writers, is one of 'already but not yet' held in tension; theirs is one of 'already' with little room for 'not yet.' Having received the Spirit, they have already arrived; for them spirituality means to have been transported into a whole new sphere of existence where they are 'above' the earthly, and especially 'fleshly,' existence of others."[11]

Fee continues:

> "The Corinthians' pride in spiritual status apparently included a degree of embarrassment over Paul's lack thereof, not to mention his lack of wisdom and eloquence. It was perhaps doubtful from their perspective whether he was an apostle with much standing. With a final thrust at this pride he affirms not only that he is like one condemned to die in the arena, but that the spectacle is for the whole world to behold."[12]

The Corinthians' version of over-realized eschatology made no room for a theology of weakness. They failed to understand the manifold ways God uses weakness in the life of the believer to magnify Himself. Perhaps someone you know is a modern version. This person might be unusually positive, upbeat, and triumphant, to a fault. She is all about miracles and overcoming and is usually the best person to be around, until, well, she isn't. When catastrophe strikes in your life and you're feeling like Job, she can't acknowledge your suffering. However, she will continue the pep talks and insist on tying a metaphorical red bow and inspirational quote around the entire disastrous situation. She can be frustrating, if not borderline delusional. Someone with an over-realized eschatology often assumes everyone living faithfully will be visibly thriving. Paul's ministry is a devastating argument against this assumption. For a follower of the crucified Christ, not everything is as it seems, for "God chose the foolish things of the world to shame the wise; God chose the weak things of the world to shame the strong" (1 Cor. 1:27, NIV).

The scandal of the cross is the primary lens through which Paul viewed his apostleship.

All of this is why Timothy had to go to Corinth and remind the fledgling church of Paul's way of life. But if Paul's authority was being challenged in Corinth—if Paul's eloquence was being called into question—how concerned must he have been for this younger, less-experienced man he loves like his son? And indeed Paul was quite concerned. At the end of the letter, he says:

> "When Timothy comes, see that you put him at ease among you, for he is doing the work of the Lord, as I am. So let no one despise him. Help him on his way in peace, that he may return to me, for I am expecting him with the brothers."
> 1 Cor. 16:10-11, ESV

So let no one despise him. Am I the only one who finds that language jarring? What was Timothy walking into? The New Testament doesn't tell us the outcome of Timothy's visit to Corinth. However, we know from 2 Corinthians that Paul ultimately had to send Titus to Corinth, too, (2 Cor. 7:5-16) and that Titus was successful to some extent in reconciling Paul and the congregation. I don't want to speculate, but I do hope I get the details about Timothy's trip to Corinth after Jesus returns.

As we close, I leave you with a challenge. As you read 2 Timothy closely over the coming weeks, ask yourself often, "What kind of Christianity is Paul leaving Timothy with?" Among other things, we are going to find—in stark contrast to some of the Corinthians who considered themselves kings—that for Paul the crown was still a future reality (2 Tim. 4:8). Before that glorious moment, he was going to be poured out as an offering, like the crucified one he followed.

Day Five

LEFT AND FOUND

FLASH FORWARD: *May the Lord grant mercy to the household of Onesiphorus, because he often refreshed me and was not ashamed of my chains.*
2 TIMOTHY 1:16

I get a Texas history lesson from Keith Moore almost every day. Thirty-eight years into our marriage, he's still trying to make peace with the fact that I wasn't born here. I'm the first transplant to marry into his family since they settled in these sweltering parts and, by doggies, he'll not have me both ill-bred and uninformed. Think of me as the Texas version of Eliza Doolittle. He's tutored me in every subject from the battles of the Texas Republic to the scientific names of native shrubs. My most recent lesson was on livestock wherein I learned that men of the Texas frontier originally experimented with camels as an alternative to horses. It's hard to picture bandana-clad cowboys galloping across the plains of the wild, wild West on the backs of camels. We should be equally glad, on this wild frontier of faith, that God saw fit for some of our plans not to succeed. I'm hoping that truth gets somebody over the hump today.

> We should be glad, on this wild frontier of faith, that God saw fit for some of our plans not to succeed.

PLEASE READ 2 TIMOTHY 1:15-18 AND JOT THE FOUR VERSES IN THE BACK OF THE BOOK. Remember: Paul was almost certainly dictating this letter.

Based on the subject matter in this brief segment, how would you imagine the tone and pace of Paul's voice? *Sighs + slow then grateful*

Paul's reference to Asia in verse 15 referred to "a large part of the western segment of modern Turkey. In New Testament times its largest city was Ephesus,"[10] where Paul ministered for three years and Timothy was presently serving. Scholars virtually across the board agree that Paul is applying an acceptable form of hyperbole in his reference to "all" (HCSB, ESV) or "everyone" (NIV) who "turned away from" (HCSB, ESV) him. In 2 Timothy 4:19, he sends greetings to loyal friends in the same region so not all had turned away. You and I both know we don't have to be abandoned by everyone to feel totally forsaken.

The NIV wording cuts to the quick. "You know that everyone in the province of Asia has deserted me." The Greek verb *(apostrephō)* translated *deserted* (NIV) and *turned away from* (HCSB, ESV) is used in reference to doctrinal apostasy in 2 Timothy 4:4 and Titus 1:14. Therefore, a turning away from the gospel is likely also involved here. But this abandonment wasn't just doctrinal. This one was also personal.

CHECK 2 TIMOTHY 1:15 AGAIN. Do the words "deserted me" hit you differently than the words "turned away from me"? If so, how?

deserted me = left one to die

turned away = ashamed of me

To me, desertion paints a mental landscape decidedly more intense. The paintbrush of desertion sweeps the deserter out of the portrait entirely. We've not just been "turned away from" when we feel deserted. We've been left. When I imagine walking out a word picture of *deserting*, my feet tend to land on the noun form of that verb. We feel like we've been left in a desert, feeling alone even when we're not, feeling parched, weather-beaten, stung by scorpions, and left to the howling winds. Desertion is dramatic. Even when the stakes aren't nearly this high, it can carry the feeling of *you left me here to die.*

Desertion feels personal. It hits close enough to name names.

> This you know: All those in Asia have turned away from me, including Phygelus and Hermogenes.
> **2 TIMOTHY 1:15**

Have you ever felt deserted?

If the desertion involved more than one person—your family, for instance, or your department at work, or your small group at church—you no doubt could name several people who stood out among them in some way. Perhaps they were the ones whose betrayal cut the deepest or the last ones you'd ever have expected to abandon you. Let's try on an example that may fit in order to further embrace 2 Timothy 1:15.

Fill in the blanks from your personal experience.
That whole circle of friends turned away from me, including
_____*Bill*_____ and _____.

Can you feel it? Boy, I can.

As I try to imagine Paul dictating this portion of the letter, I wonder if perhaps he blew out a deep breath and shook his head as he bridged over to 2 Timothy 1:16. Read it to rekindle your memory. Thank God for Onesiphorus, for Paul's and for our own, "because he often refreshed me and was not ashamed of [me]."

Left and found. Not either/or, mind you. *Both.* Both were written into Paul's story and both will be written into ours. You've had people who have turned their backs on you or deserted you but you've also had those who refreshed you. Those who were not ashamed of you. Just when we're getting jaded and about to decide the world is a smoldering heap of jerks, an Onesiphorus comes along. Take a look at the meaning of the Greek term translated "refreshed."

> ἀναψύχω *anapsúchō; from aná, again, and psúchō, to breathe, wax cold. To make cool, refresh. Cooling again, refrigerating or refreshing with cool air as the body when overheated … used figuratively, meaning to refresh, to relieve when under distress (2 Tim. 1:16).*[11]

There you are, feeling like you've been left out in a desert, baked brittle by the scorching sun, and, out of nowhere it seems, God sends along a breath of fresh air wrapped in the dust of a fellow human. The beauty of it is that the person is no more perfect than you are. He or she simply fought and won a battle with selfishness.

> I have a feeling those words are stirring up a reminder of a few people who have been Onesiphorus for you when you were scorched and dry. Name them in this space and record how they refreshed you. Try to recount specifics.

James Brost
Mom
Bill
Michelle – way back in
Arcilla

PERUSE 1 CORINTHIANS 16:13-18. In the margin, record the three names Paul mentioned in verse 17.

Stephanus   fortunatus + Achaicus

Verse 18 drips from a quill dipped in joy. "For they have refreshed my spirit and yours. Therefore recognize such people." Refreshers are rare finds in this narcissistic world. They are servants of God to the scorched and thirsty, and worthy of our recognition. If your refreshers are still alive, consider how to recognize them in a way that would show them honor. You never know what God may do with the timing. Unbeknownst to anyone but Him, they may be in a desert of their own right now, in deep need of a breath of fresh air.

Refreshers are rare finds in this narcissistic world.

Spiritual Refreshers:

1. Romans 15:32

2. 1 Corinthians 16:18

3. 2 Corinthians 7:13

4. 2 Timothy 1:16

5. Philemon 7

6. Philemon 20

Six different times in his letters (see list in margin), the apostle gave sacred space to the refreshment believers can bring to one another.

How does 2 Corinthians 7:13 suggest second-hand effects of refreshment?

we get encouraged + fired up + those around us can "catch" the spirit

The way Paul referenced the family of Onesiphorus, both in 2 Timothy 1:16 and in the letter's benediction, leaves us wondering if the faithful servant had died. If so, his death had been fairly recent since he'd come to see Paul in the apostle's final chains. Whether or not Onesiphorus had passed away or was simply no longer in Ephesus, the memory of that cool breath of fresh air comforted the death-row inmate in a breezeless dungeon.

TAKE ANOTHER LOOK AT 2 TIMOTHY 1:15-18. How can you tell Onesiphorus was intent on seeing Paul?

He searched hard - it took time - he travelled to Rome

Somewhere deep inside of us lodges a longing to be earnestly searched for and found by somebody wonderful. We may try to deny it, outrun it, or anesthetize it. We may keep it well covered, strong-armed, and adequately smothered, but sometimes in the quiet or sometimes in the crowd, this longing still has a way of bubbling to the surface. It's too embedded in our nature to outgrow. Even the psalmist David, the man after God's own heart, grappled and groaned with longing.

> O Lord, all my longing is before you; my sighing is not hidden from you.
> **PSALM 38:9, ESV**

What we won't let God access will eventually abscess.

Longings held back from the light of God's Word and left inaccessible to His boundless love have a way of becoming hauntings. Satan uses them to taunt us with what we don't have, what he insists we'll never have, or what we've lost. What we won't let God access will eventually abscess. In the midst of those often unspoken longings, we yearn to know there are people who'd diligently search for us if we were missing. People who'd swim the ocean to get to us if we were stranded on an island. We want to be worth looking for. Worth not giving up on.

We've all run into people who've dropped out of our lives and heard them say, "I really wanted to catch up with you but I didn't have a way to get in touch with you." But we know better. The truth is, they didn't bother searching for us until they found us.

When was the last time you felt this way? *often + I are the problem*
not them

We get it because we've done it. We've used those same excuses. That's what makes the Onesiphoruses in our lives exceptional and refreshing. They go to the trouble. They think a person is worth the time. The inconvenience. The gulping of pride if that's what it takes.

Ephesus to Rome was a long, arduous trek. Surely a travel-weary Onesiphorus reached the city limits exhaling *finally!* Imagine the frustration of being unable then to locate the one he'd come looking for. Paul was apparently kept in chains in an undisclosed location where he was heavily guarded. We know he was permitted at least a few visitors because Luke was with him and because, later in the letter, he asked Timothy to come and bring another brother with him. Perhaps Luke the physician was allowed easier access to keep the prisoner from dying before the scheduled date of his execution. These are blanks we can't fill in with certainty.

But we can nod over this: Onesiphorus chased every lead until he found who he was looking for and, when he waltzed in the room, the Spirit of God blew a cool breeze into the sizzling desert of Paul's small prison cell.

Let this statement sink all the way to the bottom of your well of longing: you have been audaciously searched for and passionately found.

You have been audaciously searched for and passionately found.

> LORD, You have searched me and known me.
> You have encircled me;
> You have placed Your hand on me.
> This extraordinary knowledge is beyond me.
> It is lofty; I am unable to reach it.
> **PSALM 139:1,5-6**

And, while you're at it, don't give up on humanity. There are still Onesiphoruses in this world. Be one until you are found by one.

*Intro
then to 15:40*

Group Session Three

WATCH THE VIDEO—STRONG IN THE GRACE

INTRODUCTION
Today we will follow through on the promise I made to you on Day Two of this week's home-work by devoting this session entirely to 2 Timothy 1:6-7.

PART ONE: DISSECTING 2 TIMOTHY 1:6

"fan into flame" – Greek *anazopyrein* The *"pyr"* in the compound word means
"__Fire__." The *"ana"* in the compound word means "__again__."

"the gift of God" – Consider this proposal for a working definition of "gift" (*charisma*) in its singular form and present context:

The __supernatural__ __unction__ to __fulfill__
__divine__ __purpose__ during __our__ __earthly__
__tenure__.

You've got to __have__ God to __serve__ God.
   __know__
   __love__

"Prophecies have been made that Timothy has __the__ __gifts__
__for__ __ministry__ and this was officially, __recognize__
_____ when Paul and the elders laid hands on him. ... Paul is now referring to that public __validation__ of his gift as a means of encouraging Timothy during this difficult time. Reference to the public role of the elders is appropriate to the __public__ nature of 1 Timothy. ... But 2 Timothy is a __private__ __letter__, and Paul's personal role in Timothy's commissioning is appropriately mentioned there." Dr. W.D. Mounce[1]

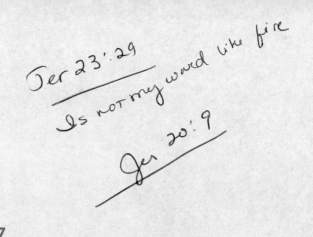

(handwritten top left)
1 Cor 12 ✻
Romans 12 ✻
1 Pet 4

(handwritten top right)
Jer 23:29
Is not my word like fire
Jer 20:9

PART TWO: DISSECTING 2 TIMOTHY 1:7

"a spirit of fear" – Greek *deilia* which means "___Cowardice___"

A spirit of fear produces ___Perversion___ . of all ___Three___
___opposing___ components:
- Perversion of power = ___Powerlessness___ or ___abuse___ of power
- Perversion of love = ___Lust___ or ___hate___
- Perversion of self-control = A ___drive___ to ___Control___ ___others___

(handwritten) Capable to seize power + use it correctly

(handwritten) Power, love, self control

(handwritten right) Holy Spirit power is Duna mis— Power

"power" in 2 Timothy 1:7– Greek *dúnamis*; Power, especially
___Achieving___ ___power___ . All the words derived from
the stem *dúna*- have the meaning of being ___able___, ___capable___ *— seized the power + use the power*
Contrast *ischús* which stresses the factuality of the ability, not necessarily the
___Accomplishment___ .

(handwritten right) Capable owous to hold—same word as used for Capture—I would have seized you

2 Timothy 1:7
ESV "self-control,"
NIV ___self discipline___,
NKJV ___sound___ ___mind___,
HCSB ___sound___ ___judgement___

"self-control" – Greek *sōphronismós;* to discipline, correct;
___Sound___ ___mind___, sober judgment.

1. W. D. Mounce, *Pastoral Epistles, Word Biblical Commentary* (Nashville, TN: Thomas Nelson, 2000), 262.

WEEK THREE

Strong in the Grace

Day One

ENTANGLED

FLASH FORWARD: *No one serving as a soldier gets entangled in the concerns of civilian life; he seeks to please the recruiter.* **2 Timothy 2:4**

When you have as many years behind you as I do, few of the mentors who significantly shaped you are still alive and kicking. Only two of mine have yet to see Jesus and both are in their early eighties. John Bisagno is one of them. He was my beloved pastor for almost twenty-five years prior to his retirement and all he taught me wouldn't fit in a book three inches thick. The other is Barbara O'Chester, a mighty woman of God who, among many other things, chaired the largest and most influential Christian women's retreat of its day. That's how I came to know her.

I got to see Barbara recently. She'd lived out of state for most of the last decade so I had not enjoyed her good company in years. Having moved back to Texas, she let me know she would be attending an upcoming Living Proof Live event. The comfort I found in her warm embrace and the familiarity of her voice as she prayed for me was palpable. She marked me deeply as a young speaker. I'd never met a woman who both *possessed* authority and *submitted* to authority the way she did. She knew who she was. She knew who she wasn't. She commanded respect. She gave respect. She knew when to stand up. She knew when to bow down. She was equal parts humble and unapologetic about her anointing.

When Barbara wasn't in her seat at the beginning of Saturday morning's session, I got a little antsy. Fifteen minutes later, I started having the most ridiculous thoughts, wondering what I might have said wrong in my teaching the night before. *And you should have worn something different, too,* I chided myself. Just before I worked myself into hives, up she walked, happy as could be. She'd simply run late. *Good grief, Beth. Get a hold of yourself.* Barbara is one of the most grace-giving people on earth. I should have known better. That moment was eye-opening for me and timely for this series. Without the fresh reminder, I might have underestimated the weight we tend to give to our mentors and spiritual mothers and fathers. That's not all bad, mind you, as long as we're not enslaved to their approval. A little fear that somebody we respect would snatch us baldheaded for misrepresenting the gospel is a mighty good thing.

OUR SECTION TODAY IS 2 TIMOTHY 2:1-7. Please read it and record it on the appropriate page. In verse 1, what did Paul call Timothy to be? _Strong_

Perhaps the hardest word in the entire New Testament to wrap our minds around is the infinitely wide one-syllable word *grace*. Defining it is not the problem. Succinctly put, grace is unmerited favor. Confining it is where we get into trouble. The truth is, we who are in Christ Jesus do not have a single challenge, need, temptation, desire, craving, conflict, sacrifice, gifting, relationship, or task where grace is limited. Further, there is no opportunity, opposition, action, or occupation where grace is ineffective. No category exists where grace is ill fit. No tank is big enough to leave grace in short supply. Grace is the divine means by which God makes Himself everything we need to utterly abound (2 Cor. 9:8). It is the medicine that heals our bitterness (Heb. 12:15). It is the floor where fallen people can come to their feet and stand (Rom. 5:2). It is substance. It is sufficiency. It is joy and felicity. And here, in 2 Timothy 2:1, grace is strength.

> *Paul used a vigorous word to express his command. To "be strong," a present passive imperative, implies that Timothy was to keep on being empowered by God (cf. 4:17; Eph 6:10; Phil 4:13; 1 Tim 1:12, where the same Greek word is used). The command demanded Timothy's continuous active cooperation with God.[1]*

The quarry from which Timothy was to mine such strength was God's grace made available in Christ Jesus.

Circle the words *keep on being empowered.*

Our tendency is to treat grace like an antibiotic. The moment we feel better, we twist the cap on tight and close the medicine cabinet on the divine supply. Soon we're just getting by instead of abounding, and soon after that we're drowning. We can't live like overcomers if we act under-graced. God's astonishing favor is meant to run like a river through every artery of our lives, but, by His sovereign plan, His unhindered access requires a cooperative process. Life is hard. Trying to be strong apart from the grace that is in Christ Jesus can be as great a tragedy as the catalyst of our need.

Where do you presently feel particularly weak right now?

always - doubt + worry about things - needs - pathetic

Grace is the divine means by which God makes Himself everything we need to utterly abound.

2 Cor 9:8 God is able to bless you abundantly, so that in all things at all times, having all that you need, you will abound in every good work

Heb 12:15 See to it that no one fails short of grace of God that no bitter root grows up to cause trouble + defile many

God specializes in granting strength in that exact area of weakness. Pause long enough to ask Him for a gush of grace from the endless spring of His provision. You have a provider who wants you to be more than a survivor. You've been entrusted with inexhaustible truth and supernatural gifting but all within the confines of borrowed time. Our days are short. Our lists are long. We need divine supply.

> **REVISIT 2 TIMOTHY 2:2.** Carefully compare it to all four of these Scriptures: 1 Timothy 1:12; 1 Timothy 2:7; 1 Timothy 1:18; and 2 Timothy 1:14. In the space below, draw a diagram of the gospel process inferred in these five verses.

$$P_{(aul)} \rightarrow T_{(im)} \rightarrow \text{(witnesses)}$$
$$\text{TO many}$$

Note the wording of 2 Timothy 2:2 in the NET.

> And entrust what you heard me say in the presence
> of many others as witnesses to faithful people who
> will be competent to teach others as well.
> 2 TIMOTHY 2:2

> Does the word *competent* jump out at you the way it jumps out at me? Explain.

As society becomes less and less inclined to acknowledge the Bible as truth, the natural propensity will be for the church to raise up fewer and fewer teachers. Here's the thing: we are not called to respond naturally. We get to see the world through the eyes of Christ and consider those bleak and unbelieving fields as white and ready for harvest (John 4:35). People long for truth. People long for answers. They long for hope. They long to believe this life is not all there is. Created in His image, humans are pre-wired with a yearning for Jesus and what He alone can bring. But, in the words of Romans 10:14, "how can they believe without hearing about Him?"

In a world less and less tolerant to truth, we get to pray earnestly to the Lord of the harvest to raise up more and more Jesus-loving, Spirit-infiltrated teachers of Scripture. Teachers who truly love people rather than platforms. Teachers who are willing to silence their phones and get off social media (I love it, too) for hours on end in order to pray hard and study diligently. Teachers, like Barbara, who are both humble and unapologetic in their

People long for answers. They long for hope. They long to believe this life is not all there is.

anointing. Jesus is looking for *faithful people who are competent to teach others.* Who on earth is up for such a task? Certainly not me. Not on my own anyway. Scripture is too precious, too sacred to be entrusted to human hands apart from the Holy Spirit.

READ 2 CORINTHIANS 3:2-6 IN EITHER THE HCSB OR NIV, IF POSSIBLE, SO YOU CAN SPOT THE WORD "COMPETENT." What does the segment say about our competency?

> *our competence comes from God*

The paradox is that we need Jesus to serve Jesus. Without Him we can do nothing that will outlast this planet's final puff of smoke. With Him, we can do the impossible, but sometimes He requires us to be willing to break a sweat.

GO BACK TO 2 TIMOTHY 2 AND FOCUS ON VERSES 4-6. List the three metaphors Paul compared to the life of a servant of Christ Jesus:

1. *Soldier* -

2. *athlete*

3. *Farmer*

What do you see as the common denominator among them?

> *Hard working — does not give up*

God is looking to raise up mighty servants He can loose all over the globe with the gospel of Jesus.

Three words: *pay the price.* I don't say those words often because sin has cost me incomparably more than obedience to Jesus has. Still, spray-painting the phrase every few miles on the pavement of this marathon could rally our resolve to reach our sweat-worthy goal. God is looking to raise up mighty servants He can loose all over the globe with the gospel of Jesus. He wants to make us profoundly and increasingly effective and bring forth tremendous fruit from our lives. He longs to enable us to do what we cannot do, love who we cannot stand, and gain what we cannot lose.

None of us will accidentally fulfill our calling. Fulfillment will require focus, stamina, self-discipline, and, as reluctant as we are to accept it, a certain amount of suffering. We have to be willing to do whatever it takes to go where God leads. Before we throw up our hands at the unreasonable prospect of this kind of focus in such frenetic times, let's find some relief in this: *entanglement does not equal involvement.* To be uninvolved with our families, our communities, our occupations, or even governmental concerns runs counter to numerous commands in Scripture.

Second Timothy 2:4 says, "No one serving as a soldier gets entangled in the concerns of civilian life; he seeks to please the recruiter." (If you are studying from an NIV84, you will see the word "involved" rather than "entangled." Be encouraged that the later addition NIV translated it "entangled" which, as you'll see in our lesson, is the far better translation of the Greek.)

Entangled is translated from the lexical Greek *emplékō: To braid in, interweave, entangle.*[2] Like me, you've probably gotten so entangled in situations and relationships, you could hardly breathe. And, also like me, you probably found that your entanglement did little, if any, long-term good. It just tied you up in the same knot you were trying to help others out of. At its noblest, entanglement is the flesh making its best attempt at playing Jesus. It germinates in the stony soil of unbalanced relationships and inappropriate expectations. Entanglement holds us hostage to unhealthy situations and demands a ransom that costs every captive dearly. If we're going to pay a price, let's make it an investment in something that guarantees eternal results. Don't think for a moment there is no prize at the end of the struggle and strain of serving Jesus Christ in a world where Christians are stranger than fiction.

GO BACK TO THOSE THREE METAPHORS IN 2 TIMOTHY 2:4-6.
Record the result of each being willing to pay the price:

1. Please the Commander

2. recieve the victory

3. 1st to recieve the crops

Keep in mind, Paul supported his ministry for years with a secular paycheck as a tentmaker. He didn't do just one thing, but everything he did was toward just one goal. He voiced his singular goal masterfully in Philippians 3:12-14.

Read the segment as today's wrap up. If it resonates with you and offers you language to simplify everything your life encompasses into one ultimate goal, record it in the space below as your own. Do it for two reasons: Because Jesus is worthy and because you, beloved, are meant to be mighty. because of the HS

I'm not close to where I think I need to be w/ Jesus but
I won't give in I know my goal

Kristen: *I'm a 30 year old who feels called to teach but I struggle with the current pull to "market one's calling" online. What advice do you have for those of us just beginning to lead/teach/disciple when it comes to allowing a community platform to organically grow versus building it online?*

Beth: *Early on, I heard the saying, "Concern yourself with the depth of your ministry and let God worry about the breadth." To this day those words ring in my ear. I ask God on a regular basis to give me swift and powerful conviction of sin when I'm crossing a line and, boy, is He faithful. The Ick Factor works effectively for me: when I'm self-promoting and self-serving, I want my insides to respond with a nauseated "Ick."*

We Believe

A half-decade ago, week after week, and for a longer time period than I expected, I shuffled alone into the back of a church where I knew no one and no one knew me. I sat on the back row, Sunday after Sunday, and, although the congregants made friendly gestures, they never said more than a word to me. I can't tell you how glad I was for that. I didn't want to talk. I didn't have anything to say, anyway. I usually sobbed quietly through most of the service. The people around me let me do that, too. They didn't try to ease the awkwardness of my agony or sign me up for a Sunday School class. They couldn't have helped me much, anyway, and they seemed to know it. It was as though they were comfortable with my pain, like somehow they knew I was in exactly the right place.

The church had a higher, more formal liturgy than I had ever experienced before. We didn't sing as much as I was accustomed to, maybe a few hymns, mostly a cappella. That was okay by me too, because, for the first time in my life I didn't have the bandwidth to stay emotionally engaged in a half-hour worship set. Hollowed out by my life circumstances, I was relieved to have made it out of bed after another sleepless night. What drew me there every week? We took communion and confessed the Nicene Creed together every Sunday.

my current circumstances or emotions. I felt like I had something solid to rest my weight on for a while, a frame sturdy enough to prop up my limp body. Repeating the creed aloud week after week gave me a concise language for my faith, centuries-old truth to confess, when I simply didn't have my own. The rhythm of the lines would ring through my mind during the week. Far from being some kind of dead ritual for me, confessing the Nicene Creed quickened something in me. I could hardly ever get to the end without losing it. Still can't.

We believe in one God,
the Father, the Almighty,
maker of heaven and earth,
of all that is, seen and unseen.[1]

We look for the resurrection
of the dead,
and the life of the world to come.
Amen.[2]

When I recited the words of the creed with saints to my right and to my left, I got the sense that my Christian faith wasn't at the mercy of

Even though I was alone all those months in the back pew, I didn't feel alone. I was confessing the gospel using the language of

entrusted

the ancient church alongside my brothers and sisters in the faith. And meanwhile, on the very same day, multitudes of other Christians all over the world were joining their voices in the same refrain. In crucial ways I felt more linked than ever by this ancient common language.

In the following paragraph, John Webster says some important things about what a creed is and is not:

> "A confession or creed is a proclamation, a publication or making known of that which is confessed. To confess is not to reflect, even to reflect theologically; it is to herald the gospel. A confessional formula, therefore, shares the vividness and directness of the act of confession by which it is generated. To confess is to testify—and to testify with a bit of noise ... A creed is not a program, a platform, a manifesto to mobilize our forces. It is an amazed cry of witness: 'Behold the Lamb of God who takes away the sin of the world!' (John 1:29, NASB) Confession is attestation, not self-assertion."[3]

The worthwhile but admittedly thorny theological conversation concerning the official creeds, like the Apostles' Creed and the Nicene Creed, and their authoritative function in the history of the church, is far beyond the scope of this excerpt. It is, however, important to note that while I believe the confession of creeds is important and hope it is an act that enjoys widespread practice, I am not elevating any of the historic creeds to the level of authoritative Scripture. On the contrary, as Webster says: "a confession binds insofar as it is in agreement with Holy Scripture: it binds by saying 'Scripture says'. As with all instruments of the church's order, the authority of the creed is inseparable from its submission to the Word of God; it has the authority of the herald, not the magistrate."[4]

I want to shift from referring to creeds in an official sense to discuss the early creedal statements we find in the New Testament text.

While there is no official "creed" in the text of the New Testament, there are the beginnings of creedal-type statements or fragments of creedal statements.

These creedal statements range from the simple assertion "Jesus is Lord" (Rom. 10:9) to lengthier assertions such as Paul's clarification of the gospel in 1 Corinthians 15:3-5.[5] They are concise statements that sum up "the heart of Christian faith."[6]

Because the earliest Christians were actual human beings like you and me, these statements did not arise in a vacuum but were prompted by actual situations in the life of the earliest church. For example, many think the confessions were used during the church's baptism ceremonies as a requirement for potential church members.[7] But a number of other real-life situations, such as preaching, apologetics, and a variety of liturgical scenarios such as hymns and prayers,[8] could have also prompted creedal statements.

Well, friend, there is much more to say about these matters, so I hope you'll join me again in the next article! We'll pick up right where we are leaving off. Wishing joy and peace to you today wherever you are on your road home.

Day Two

THE BOUNDLESS
WORD OF GOD

FLASH FORWARD: *I suffer for it to the point of being bound like a criminal, but God's message is not bound.* **2 Timothy 2:9**

Day One concluded with Paul's singular life-goal poignantly engraved on the scroll in Philippians 3:12-14. Read the segment again from the NIV in the margin.

Those three verses can tell you more about the nature of a divine calling than the combined advice of a dozen mentors.

> **List everything the segment infers about calling:**
>
> it is ever evolving
> continue to strain, learn, pray to move forward
> forgive your past — let it go so you can move forward
> there is a goal + a prize
> all of this because Jesus grabbed me first + just as
> I was — deformed + ugly, weak + powerless —

My good friend Janice began working as a courier for the TV broadcast department of a major ministry in her late teens. Basically, her job was to pick stuff up and drop stuff off. Over time she became a production assistant for the TV show and then shifted into floor directing. Her supervisors eventually started letting her try her hand at producing a few pieces for the program. Impressed, it wasn't long until they made her a full-fledged producer. When few others were available to go into countries to eyewitness terrific suffering as part of the ministry's outreach, she said she'd go. Sixty-eight countries later, Janice is an international photographer and has done more to spotlight the needs of suffering children and bring them aid than anyone I know. The woman had no earthly idea what Jesus wanted to do with her. She just kept showing up and working hard at whatever He put in front of her. She's never married. Never had a baby. But she has children of every color all over the world.

Not that I have already obtained all this, or have already arrived at my goal, but I press on to take hold of that for which Christ Jesus took hold of me. Brothers and sisters, I do not consider myself yet to have taken hold of it. But one thing I do: Forgetting what is behind and straining toward what is ahead, I press on toward the goal to win the prize for which God has called me heavenward in Christ Jesus.

PHILIPPIANS 3:12-14, NIV

Welcome to the Jesus journey. A few things you may have noted in Philippians 3:12-14:

1) VERSE 12A: *Not that I have already reached the goal or am already fully mature ...*

Your calling is continually in process and under construction. It's not something you obtain by a certain age and then maintain. Get over thinking that you're supposed to have arrived at your goal by now. Just keep walking it out with Jesus.

2) VERSE 12B: *... but I make every effort to take hold of it ...*

Your calling will require stretching your full length forward, straining, reaching, and pressing to take the next piece of ground.

3) VERSE 12C: *... because I have been taken hold of by Christ.*

Your calling is "to take hold of that for which Christ Jesus took hold of [you]." You don't even have to know for certain what it is. All you need to know is that He knows. He'll show you as you go. You may not be able to give it a name until your race is nearly over. Until then, your calling is *whatever*—whatever He put in front of you right now.

4) VERSE 13: *Brothers, I do not consider myself to have taken hold of it. But one thing I do: Forgetting what is behind and reaching forward to what is ahead ...*

Your calling is not behind you. It's in front of you. Forget yesterday—both the failures and the fabulous—and move on. Nothing can mess up tomorrow like hanging onto yesterday. If you've begged God for years to engage you in your calling, yet feel He's never responded, it may be that you're having trouble facing forward. Ask Him to shed light on the delay.

> Your calling is not behind you. It's in front of you.

5) VERSE 14: *... I pursue as my goal the prize promised by God's heavenly call in Christ Jesus.*

Lastly, you'll cross the finish line of your calling when God calls you to heaven. Your prize is there.

Which one of the five speaks loudest to you right now and why?

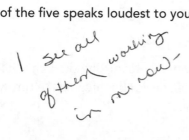

I see all of them working in me now-

The gorgeousness is that all five are adaptable and applicable to every season, whether you're in high school, college, single, married, divorced, widowed, middle age, or in your eighties. They apply whether God presently has you behind a desk, on the basketball court, in assisted living, changing diapers, cleaning teeth, building websites or high rises. *Here I am, Lord. What do You want me to take hold of here?* If He has nothing for you there—no preparation, equipping, serving, exemplifying, or testifying of any kind—you're in the wrong place and it's His responsibility to move you. Welcome Him to and be faithful until He does.

On to 2 Timothy!

> **PLEASE READ 2 TIMOTHY 2:8-13 AND WRITE THE SEGMENT IN THE BACK OF YOUR BOOK.** In verse 8, Paul worded the gospel in short-form to Timothy, featuring only two aspects of the life of Christ. What were they?

Raised from the dead AND Descended from David

At first blush, the two comprise an incomplete equation for the sum of the gospel, but used as headings, virtually every vital element of Christ's story can be categorized beneath them. To be raised from the dead, Jesus had to live and die and defy the laws of nature. His bodily resurrection sets Him apart from every other religious figure in history. No stone marked His bones. No cave stayed His grave. Jesus alone conquered death.

The second heading often loses its prominence when we with Gentile backgrounds share the gospel story. For the Jews, no other qualification mattered if one rumored to be the Messiah were not a descendant of David. In 2 Samuel 7, God promised David through the prophet Nathan that He'd raise up a descendant whose kingdom would never end. Though David's son, Solomon, would sit upon the throne and build the temple, his reign would cease and his body would rot like every other king who followed him. The prophecy was about Christ. Romans 1:1-4 puts a little more meat around the short-form gospel found in 2 Timothy 2:8.

> **READ ROMANS 1:1-4** and record additional elements that stand out to you. The Gospel of God — that stands out — I have always thought of the Gospel as the story of grace thru Jesus — descendant of David physically but a HS appointed son of God

Lici is on my Living Proof Live worship team. She sits right on the front row during the teaching sessions and constantly threatens to throw a shoe when she hears something good from the Scriptures. Second Timothy 2:9 turns me into Lici. It makes me want to throw a shoe like nobody's business.

Rewrite Paul's point in your own words: *God's word is not bound by our @physical bodies it is HS inspired - delivered - implanted - taught - evolving - moving + POWERFUL*

You can bind and gag the messenger but you cannot bind or gag the message. You can set the feet of the preacher on fire but you can't stamp out the gospel he preached. You can cut the tongues out of a thousand Bible teachers but you cannot silence the mouth of God. You can confiscate every page of Scripture in a closed country and the Spirit will see to it that others are smuggled in. You can chain up every Christian on the planet but God's Word cannot be chained. You can mute your TV, your phone, and your laptop but you cannot mute God. Build a wall—He'll walk right through it. Pour a moat and He'll walk on top of it. Block Him with a mountain and He'll command it to move.

My word that comes from My mouth will not return to Me empty, but it will accomplish what I please and will prosper in what I send it to do.
ISAIAH 55:11 *Woo Hoo*

According to 2 Timothy 2:10, why did Paul endure all things? *FOR ME!! Thank you Paul*

When life doesn't seem worth living or feels like too much to bear, courage can come from setting our sights beyond our own plights to the hope of salvation and deliverance for others. Your faithfulness is the key to somebody else's faith. Nothing about outward focus during inward pain is natural but it could well be our survival. Self-focus would have killed Paul long before his execution date. If you and I want to lie down and die long before we're dead, being self-consumed in our season of suffering should do the trick. But that's not what we really want. There is iron in the blood of Jesus and it runs through our spiritual veins.

> Your faithfulness is the key to somebody else's faith.

We've arrived at the point in Paul's second letter to Timothy where his conversational writing style took a brief but dramatic detour. Read 2 Timothy 2:10-13 aloud if possible and you'll easily recognize the shift. Can you hear the text suddenly take on a syncopated rhythm in verses 11-13? Numerous scholars suggest Paul may have quoted several lines from a hymn of the early church. If so, don't you wonder how the tune went? Or if the early worshipers stuck with the melody or broke out into harmony? Imagining how Christ's incarnation altered the wording in the worship of those first Jewish Christians completely intrigues me. Their hymns had been set in stone for centuries. If these thoughts intrigue you, too, you'll want to read Melissa's articles this week on creeds. I think you'll love them.

Here's something else: if verses 11-13 are extractions from a hymn, it is even possible Paul wrote it.

> Compare verse 11 to Romans 6:8, and record the concept they have in common.
>
> *If we died to Christ, He lives in us thru HS*

> Which line of the hymn in verses 11-13 issues an unsettling warning?
>
> *If we deny Christ - He will also deny us*

> Which line do you find most relieving and encouraging?
>
> *If we are faithless He will remain faithful*

I could try my hand at writing a summation of 2 Timothy 2:11-13 until my wrist snapped and still not make it as crisp and clean and clear as Dr. Mounce has done in the excerpt below.

> Mark it up, circling the key word he uses to begin each of the four points and underlining everything else you find helpful.

Paul concludes with a magnificent hymn, which regardless of origin speaks directly to Timothy and his historical situation and includes a strong eschatological emphasis. (1) Conversion: those who have died with Christ in their conversion/baptism will live with Christ in their post-conversion life (sanctification). (2) Perseverance: if during their lives as believers they continue to be faithful to God and persevere, then they will surely reign with Christ in heaven. (3) Apostasy: however, if some deny Christ, if through their lives they deny knowing him by their word and deed, then before the judgment seat Christ will also deny knowing them. (4) Faithlessness: however, if a believer fails to persevere fully but yet stops short of apostasy, God will remain true to his character, true to his promises, and therefore will remain faithful to that person (immutability of God).[3]

God remains faithful. Heaven help us, where would we be if He didn't? Through the pages of this study, He is beckoning us to also remain faithful, not in our own strength but His. God charges us with utmost seriousness to be trustworthy with the treasures He's entrusted to us. That is our aim. To that we give our all. And when we fail and falter in our faith, as we surely will at times, this we hold tight to our chests in our fears and tears: "He remains faithful, for He cannot deny Himself."

Day Three

GOD-APPROVAL

FLASH FORWARD: *Be diligent to present yourself approved to God, a worker who doesn't need to be ashamed, correctly teaching the word of truth.*
2 Timothy 2:15

You can't please everybody. Maybe some people learn that lesson without getting all bruised up. Maybe others get bruised black and blue, but at least they learned the lesson once and for all. I was in neither category. I fell into the endurance test group where I picture angels with clipboards collecting data for a survey based on this question: "How many beatings can one person take until she's/he's finally weaned from approval addiction?" Sometimes weaning from an addiction requires wounding by the addiction. It has to do us so wrong that we come to hate it.

› Drugs alcohol gluttony

I wanted to please people in the worst way and I do mean the whole lot of them. Every camp in Christianity. Every person I taught. My leaders, my friends, my coworkers, and God knows I wanted to please my mother. I adored her and delighted in her favor. I'd still like to have the ongoing approval of my husband and daughters but I gave that up as a core value about the time a specialist predicted the removal of part of my intestines. The three of us—my intestines and I—are significantly happier.

> Have these things also been a battle for you? If so, when was the last time you tasted how toxic the desire for human approval and affirmation could be? Explain.
>
> *I still want to please so I am "Careful" how I witness + by that I water down the Gospel - Shame on me -*

PLEASE READ 2 TIMOTHY 2:14-18 AND RECORD IT IN THE BACK OF THE BOOK.

To become mighty servants of God—our journey's aim—we have to be loosed from the approval of man and our insatiable lust for human affirmation. We long for somebody to say to us, *well done*. Whether we seek those two words through performance or appearance, left to our natural selves, we all crave them. Mutual encouragement is biblical and not on the chopping block today. However, seeking man's approval is outsourcing our identities to fellow humans who are as selfish, short-sighted, and fickle as we. It's pedaling a bike in front of a freight train. Eventually it will run over us. It's perilous even if the person from whom we seek approval and affirmation is righteous. In John 5:44, Jesus called out an impressively religious group of people with these words: "While accepting glory from one another, you don't seek the glory that comes from the only God." The issue is that we cannot serve two masters. We become a slave to the person we seek most to please.

that's me!

I'd like to go on record saying that, on most occasions, I find God infinitely easier to please than man. In fact, He alone knows how much of my disobedience along the way stemmed from being willing to displease Him rather than my fellow man simply because He was more merciful. That's not the mark of a mighty servant. That's the mark of a coward.

Second Timothy 2:14 says,

> Be diligent to present yourself approved to God, a worker who doesn't need to be ashamed …

The words "well done" are on the tip of Jesus' tongue. I think He can hardly wait to say them. He's not manipulative. He's not moody. He tells us what He wants and He tells us how He'll respond. He never departs from His Word.

> … correctly teaching the word of truth.

Our means of knowing the gospel so well it rolls off our tongues is studying the living, breathing brilliance of Him in the sacred pages.

I'm throwing down this gauntlet throughout our series: we may not all be called to teach but we are all called to be profoundly effective communicators of the gospel. Whether or not you've stepped into this measure of your calling, you have a Christian communicator down inside of you and a gifted one at that. My earnest prayer is that God will use these five weeks to surface that gifting with a strength, an anointing, and effectiveness beyond what you've yet experienced. Our means of knowing the gospel so well it rolls off our tongues is studying the living, breathing brilliance of Him in the sacred pages. Scholar Thomas C. Oden gets specific in his commentary on 2 Timothy:

> "Correct handling" is an artisan's metaphor that suggests a skilled craftsman building in accurate plumb line with steady skill. The right handling of the word of truth must begin by gratefully receiving the New Testament as the only written testimony we have to the most crucial events in human history. It attests to God's own ministry to the world, God's own coming, God's own acting within the life and ministry of Jesus

to accomplish his mission through the Son and Holy Spirit. ... There is an aesthetic dimension to the metaphor of the skilled artisan. The worker is justly proud of work well done and is happy to submit it for the inspection of the master. Neither lazy nor careless, the worker has no reason to be ashamed of his work.[4]

Correctly handling the Scriptures won't come naturally to any of us. Interpreting the Bible by our experiences and preferences is our natural inclination. Anyone who avoids the tendency does so on purpose. Stop short of assuming that correct teaching and personal illustration can never coexist. Jesus illustrated truth continually through parables. You don't have to keep your personality out of your ministry. Paul's description of his approach in 1 Thessalonians 2:8 is spectacular.

> You don't have to keep your personality out of your ministry.

What two things did he, Timothy, and Silvanus share with the Thessalonians?

Gospel + their lives

Perhaps God's confidence in the durability of His Word is nowhere more blatant than in His willingness to place it into the fleshly palms of flawed people. Every teacher, every student, every preacher, and every processor of the Word of God gets it wrong at times. Every communicator miscommunicates on occasion. To minimize the frequency, let's ...

... **STAY TENDER TO THE CONVICTION OF THE HOLY SPIRIT.** Pay attention to that nudging inside of you asking in various words, "Are you sure about that?"

... **CONSULT WELL-RECOMMENDED RESOURCES.** If you're a teacher, that includes but is not limited to Bible commentaries. Rogue may be en vogue but what's sound has been around. One of the best pieces of advice I ever received from my mentor? "Beth, this Book has been studied for thousands of years. If you come up with an interpretation nobody else has, assume you're wrong." Dr. Oden points out a Greek word in 2 Timothy 2:15 that has an important English cousin: "The metaphor of rightly dividing (*orthotomeo*) the word of truth, with which our term orthodoxy is cognate, implies straight, precise, careful transmission of the word of truth, the gospel."[5] Creative with illustrations. Orthodox with interpretations.

... **STAY TEACHABLE UNDER THE COUNSEL AND CORRECTION OF WISE PEOPLE WITH *OPEN ACCESS TO US*.**

Who gets to correct you without you getting defensive? Write his or her name below.

Frieda
our
Pastor

If you don't have anyone, find someone.

... STAY IN THE LOOP. Nothing is more dangerous than a teacher, preacher, or communicator who refuses to listen to others teach, preach, and communicate. Secure people want to be inspired and sharpened by others. Insecure people can't take the competition. Those who only like the sound of their own voices will sooner or later slide into lies. Isolation invites deception. Likewise, Bible students are smart to study under multiple teachers so they don't blindly follow one teacher into a doctrinal ditch.

... DON'T QUICKLY DISMISS THE QUESTIONS AND COMPLAINTS OF YOUR CRITICS. If the shoe fits, let's stick our sore toes in it as much as we hate to and adjust how we walk.

TWO QUESTIONS BASED ON THE PREVIOUS SUGGESTIONS:

Which suggestions have you learned on your own through memorable personal experience? Explain how. *HS nudge — listen !!.!*
Multiple teachers (Irida even encourages this)

Have I overlooked a safeguard you'd like to add? If so, please do.
Watch your emotions— If you are ever inspired to follow a crowd — check yourself with prayer right away.
We are going to save our comments on Paul's exhortation "not to fight about words" (v. 14) until Day Five since it bears similarities to verses at the end of the chapter. Let's put a lovely bow on today's lesson with the gangrene of Hymenaeus and Philetus. I Googled the condition and trust me when I tell you we don't want it. You have never seen grimier toes than the gangrenous sort. No pedicure on the ever-loving earth will offset all that charcoal black, green, and yellow. Furthermore, the toenail will pop off with the first file. But don't take my word for it. Here's an official definition:

gan•grene
[Latin *gangraena*, from Greek *gangraina*; akin to Greek *gran* to gnaw] 1543
1: local death of soft tissues due to loss of blood supply
2: pervasive decay or corruption: ROT

Don't even get me started on gangrene's kinship to the Greek word for gnaw.

How had Hymenaeus and Philetus deviated from the truth?
They taught that when Jesus rose from the dead that was the end — resurrection complete

We'll invite Dr. Oden to the podium one last time today:

> They saw everything in the Christian proclamation as pointing to something that had happened, without seeing this as impinging upon the present and the future. The key to the death and resurrection of Christ is not that it is just a past event but that the living Lord is present in our midst, interceding for us, and will appear in the end of history … Hymenaeus and Philetus had erred on more than an incidental point; it was the most basic point of the Christian kerygma—resurrection teaching. They did not deny the resurrection altogether but interpreted it so as to take away its power and reality, namely, by saying that the resurrection was exclusively and simply past. They may have viewed the resurrection allegorically, as a spiritual resurrection only and not a bodily resurrection.[6]

What part of Dr. Oden's excerpt speaks loudest to you?

none

Please tolerate one last commentary excerpt because this from Matthew Henry is irresistible:

> The resurrection of the dead is one of the great doctrines of Christ. Now see the subtlety of the serpent and the serpent's seed. They did not deny the resurrection (for that had been boldly and avowedly to confront the word of Christ), but they put a corrupt interpretation upon that true doctrine, saying that the resurrection was past already, that what Christ spoke concerning the resurrection was to be understood mystically and by way of allegory, that it must be meant of a spiritual resurrection only. It is true, there is a spiritual resurrection, but to infer thence that there will not be a true and real resurrection of the body at the last day is to dash one truth of Christ in pieces against another. By this they overthrew the faith of some, took them off from the belief of the resurrection of the dead; and if there be no resurrection of the dead, nor future state, no recompence of our services and sufferings in another world, we are of men the most miserable, 1 Corinthians 15:19.[7]

Diligently studying Scripture increasingly guards us against *dashing one truth of Christ in pieces against another*. So, keep it up and learn from many teachers. And while you're at it, smile a little. No need to be *of men the most miserable*, fellow student of Scripture. Rest assured and rejoice in hope. Jesus who died was raised to life. He is the firstfruit of the resurrection (1 Cor. 15:20-22). The guarantee of our destiny. When you lay your lifeless body down, no doctrine of men or demon of hell has the power to hold you down with it.

Day Four

EVERYONE AND ANYONE

FLASH FORWARD: *Nevertheless, God's solid foundation stands firm, having this inscription: The Lord knows those who are His, and Everyone who names the name of the Lord must turn away from unrighteousness.* 2 Timothy 2:19

Let's just go ahead and start this lesson by pulling back the bowstring and aiming a razor-sharp arrow straight at the heart of one of our deepest worries: we're unsure if some of our loved ones are in Christ. Sometimes we think they are. Sometimes we think they're not. If you're like me, sometimes you think they are because you cannot bear to think they're not.

> Which loved one leaps most quickly to your mind as we launch this discussion? Why has this individual's relationship to Jesus been so difficult to figure out? *michael— He talks like his close + about to leap but then backs up + does not limit — Bill says one thing does another*

In all likelihood, my answer would in some way overlap yours. Sometimes my lean toward hope has less to do with evidences of their faith than it does with the extravagant mercies of Jesus. Never once in the Gospels, no matter how grave the trespass, did He turn away a sinner who didn't deny the sin. Jesus didn't come to rally the righteous. He came to save sinners. He was named for such a purpose. Take a glance at Matthew 1:20-21.

> Exactly why was Joseph to give the son of Mary, conceived in her by the Holy Spirit, the name *Jesus*?
>
> Because He will ... *Save His people from their sins*

Saving people from their sins is what Jesus came to do. The physician came for the sick (Mark 2:17). Jesus hotly contested those who considered themselves too righteous and religious to admit their need. Yet even at the apex of His agony on the cross, He prayed for those who nailed Him to that tree, "Father, forgive them, because they do not know what they are doing" (Luke 23:34).

That is mercy. That same merciful Savior also told people to turn from their sins (John 5:14; 8:11). Here in this tension we begin our lesson.

PLEASE READ 2 TIMOTHY 2:19-22 AND HANDWRITE THE SEGMENT ON THE APPROPRIATE PAGE.

Nevertheless, God's solid foundation stands firm. Feeling the weightiness of that statement requires recapturing our context. Glance at the section preceding today's verses and review the epidemic of heresies in Ephesus and how false teachers were undermining faith. The nevertheless certainty? Should heresies all the more increase, God's foundation would be never the less secure. Nothing and no one could crack, crumble, or melt to lava the rock-solid foundation upon which His household would be built. The New Testament is ground to more than a few building metaphors and several blueprints come from Paul's own pen. The apostle's emphasis varies from context to context so the metaphors don't offer identical interpretations. At the same time, they are not difficult to reconcile.

Record in the blanks the identity of the house and the layered foundation including the cornerstone, according to the verses below.

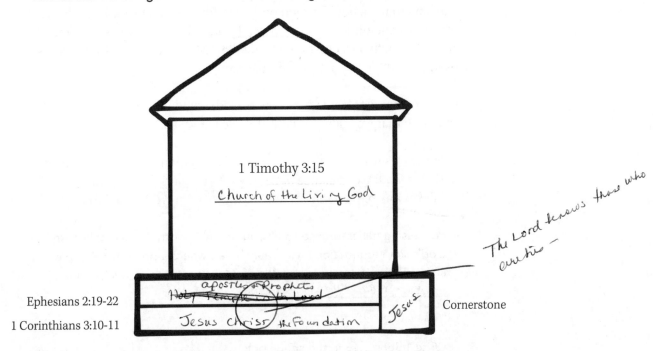

1 Timothy 3:15

Church of the Living God

The Lord knows those who are his —

apostles & prophets

Holy Temple in the Lord

Ephesians 2:19-22

1 Corinthians 3:10-11

Jesus Christ the Foundation   Jesus   Cornerstone

In 2 Timothy 2:19, the foundation is "sealed with this inscription"—literally, "having this seal" *(echōn tēn sphragida tautēn).* A seal declared the official ownership and authenticity of a structure or document. Affixed on a document, it was similar to the presidential seal, the official coat of arms, authenticating a letter from the Oval Office to the United States Congress.

The seal in 2 Timothy 2:19 was depicted on a structure and contained two inscriptions.

> As a representation, return to the graphic and draw one circle at the midpoint of the layered foundation right on top of the blanks you filled in with "Jesus Christ" and "the apostles and prophets." Draw two lines extending from the circle to the margin. Record each inscription from 2 Timothy 2:19 there.

To follow Jesus closely is to fulfill your calling completely.

"The Lord knows those who are His." Thank God He does. Thank God He doesn't sit there rubbing His chin trying to figure out if we belong to Him or not. Whom the Holy Spirit conceives, the Holy Spirit claims. We may at times be half-hearted but at no time are we half-breeds. Those born of the Spirit are the children of God by the will of God (John 1:11-13; 3:3-6). He has no unwanted sons or daughters. When He called your name, He didn't rattle it off mindlessly with a million others or butcher the pronunciation like the school teacher with a new roll. God knew you before He formed Adam from the dust. He called your name with passion and anticipation. Since before you were born, He's been preparing you and working in you, "enabling you both to desire and to work out His good purpose" (Phil. 2:13). The path toward your destiny was not hidden. It was driven through the soil by the south end of a cross. "Take up [your] cross daily and follow Me" (Luke 9:23). To follow Jesus closely is to fulfill your calling completely.

Dr. Gordon Fee words our great relief: "God's building rests not on the shaky foundation that we know God but that He knows us."[8]

But our ankles will be shaky on that solid foundation if we doubt where we stand with God. We will never be a threat to the darkness or a menace to the devil if we can't settle in our minds whether or not we are in Christ.

> Possessing full assurance to fill your name in both these blanks turns God's solid foundation into a launch pad where a powerful life takes liftoff: The Lord knows _____ Me, Ramona _____ is His and _____ I - Ramona _____ knows she/he is His.

> Write 1 John 5:13 in the space below. (Paul is directly talking to us
> I write these things to you 2000 some years ago) who believe in the name of Jesus so that you may know you have eternal life

Our confidence level will vacillate unnervingly if we sub the word *knows* with *thinks* or *feels*.

FLIP OVER TO EPHESIANS 6 AND PERUSE THE PIECES OF THE ARMOR OF GOD IN VERSES 10-17. Which piece of armor includes the word *salvation*?

A helmet does one thing. It protects the head. Your mind's most fundamental protection in this warp and woof existence is your unwavering confidence that you are a blood-bought child of God. If you are in Christ, you are saved. It doesn't matter how you feel. It doesn't matter what your temporary numbness or sudden surge of fear suggests. You are saved. And you know it. This side of the veil, there is so much we do not know. Let's know this. Have you received Jesus as your personal Savior? Have you believed in your heart and confessed with your mouth that Jesus is Lord? Have you turned from your own way and forsaken all other means of salvation to accept the free gift of grace God offered to you through the cross of Christ? Then tighten the strap to that helmet of salvation and save your doubts for lesser things. In the words of Acts 2:21, "everyone who calls on the name of the Lord will be saved."

As well, "Everyone who names the name of the Lord must turn away from unrighteousness" (2 Tim. 2:19). We know from Scripture that believers can be seduced by the enemy from their pure-hearted devotion to Christ (2 Cor. 11:2-3). We know that, under pressure and duress, followers of Jesus can foolishly claim not to know Him and yet still be restored and put to work for the kingdom (Luke 22:31-34). We know that true brothers and sisters in Christ can fall into sin and that even the spiritual among us are warned to be careful lest, in trying to help them up, they are also tempted (Gal. 6:1).

But we also know "if we say, 'We don't have any sin,' we make Him a liar, and His word is not in us" (1 John 1:10). If we can long endure in our unrighteousness, undisturbed and unrepentant, something is wrong. This condition differs from cycling in and out of sin in a loop of sin-misery-repentance-restoration, repeat. However, we can also be loosed from that dizzying loop. Such was my pattern in adolescence and young adulthood. Same sin, seven hundredth time with a holy hiatus in between that wore off with the next tidal wave of temptation. Sound familiar at all? What throws a question mark on whether or not an individual is truly in Christ is his or her ability to stay indefinitely in a stronghold of sin, free of conviction and unmoved to repentance. The Holy Spirit convicts us of sin and, if He dwells in us, He does His job.

THE HOLY SPIRIT'S JOB IS EXPRESSED MAGNIFICENTLY IN 2 CORINTHIANS 3:18. Word it here.

Paul reminded the young pastor of the church in Ephesus that those "who name the name of the Lord must turn away from unrighteousness." We *must.*

Q & A

Valerie: *To love at all is to be vulnerable. With that being said, how can a leader in ministry acquire thicker skin but not a harder heart?*

Beth: *The only way we won't get hurt is to withdraw our hearts but withdrawing our hearts will sooner or later withdraw our effectiveness. In Paul's wording, "our heart has been opened wide." (2 Cor.6:11) We have to fight to keep it that way. Our first big wave of maturity in leadership is usually a crash course in conflict and hurt. A certain amount comes with the territory but all of it can be used by God to grow us and teach us dependency. Perhaps the armor of God in Ephesians 6 is our replacement for thick skin. We keep our hearts wide open and our armor on tight.*

For example — Lie + you have to continue the Lie —
it becomes a cage of sorts /
i.e. hitting grow up & pray for
i.e. I don't even want to
put this life by lie on
paper —

Our God is holy. Every drop of His Son's blood was crimson gold to Him, costly beyond human calculation. Our God is also wise. He knows what sets our souls up to prosper and we do not prosper in sin. At first, sin appears to befriend us, but, over time, it drops the mask to reveal a demanding bully blackmailing and betraying us. The God-confidence we need to advance in our calling gets undermined and we backtrack into that same doubt. We hand a microphone to our accuser who taunts and interrogates us. "How can you be a real Christian? You're such a hypocrite. Who are you to serve God?" I learned the hard way that God's insistence on our turning from sin is not at the opposite end of the divine spectrum from His attribute of mercy. It is a mercy all its own.

> So if anyone purifies himself from anything dishonorable,
> he will be a special instrument, set apart, useful to
> the Master, prepared for every good work.
> 2 TIMOTHY 2:21

Did you catch the word *anyone*? Circle it.

Anyone includes you, me, and every person we love and long to be in Christ and instrumental in the kingdom of God.

Note the condition Paul emphasized for being a special instrument: "if anyone purifies himself from anything ___dishonorable___."

Where God's will appears to confine us we are paradoxically and ultimately freed.

One of the widest eye-openers we experience in our process of sanctification is that anything dishonorable to God is also dishonorable to us. To treat Him with respect also treats you with respect. His honor is our dignity. God is not trying to cheat us out of worldly pleasures. He's trying to keep worldly pleasures from cheating us. The perimeters of His will are not in place to limit us. They are to keep our flesh and our unseen foe from limiting us. Where God's will appears to confine us we are paradoxically and ultimately freed.

So, Paul writes to Timothy, flee from youthful passions, and pursue ___righteousness___, ___faith___, ___love___ and ___peace___, along with those who call on the Lord from a pure heart (2 Tim. 2:22). (Fill in the blanks.)

Try to name one among the four pursuits that is toxic, diminishing, perverse, humiliating, or belittling to us and our tongues will stick to the roofs of our mouths in dry silence. God's will is our good.

Righteousness, faithfulness, love, and *peace*: the four-part harmony of one whole life.

Paul's Use of Traditions

In Day Two of this week's homework you studied what is perhaps my favorite section in all of 2 Timothy: chapter 2, verses 8-13.

The section begins with this strong and concise statement: "Remember Jesus Christ, raised from the dead, descended from David. This is my gospel" (NIV). Mom had you read Romans 1:1-4 alongside it because the two passages have marked similarities as a short-form of the gospel. In addition, both Romans 1:1-4 and 2 Timothy 2:8 are considered by many scholars to be fragments of creedal formulae.[9] The concentration of such important terms such as "remember," "Jesus Christ" (in that order, as opposed to "Christ Jesus"), "raised from the dead," and "descended from David," and the fact that almost none of these terms are used again in precisely the same way in 2 Timothy point to the strong possibility that 2 Timothy 2:8 was used by the early church to sum up their faith. Mom also mentioned how verses 11-13 are considered by most scholars to be a hymn of the early church.

If we have died with him,
we will also live with him;
if we endure, we will also reign
with him;
if we deny him, he will also deny us;
if we are faithless, he remains faithful,
for he cannot deny himself.
2 Timothy 2:11b-13, ESV

Distinguishing between creedal formulas that were used to help teach new converts and hymns that were used in the church liturgy is not an easy task and may not be totally necessary since their function overlaps.[10] As J.L. Wu says: "In origin and usage, hymnic materials and creedal confessions are essentially the same, that is, they were originally devised for evangelistic, cultic, apologetic purposes and carried didactic and hortative functions in their contexts."[11] While their function is similar, scholars sometimes determine traditions are hymns and not creedal confessions based on: 1) syntactical features such as introductory relative pronouns in the Greek text and 2) style, whether written in poetic or metrical style.

Of course we don't have any audio recording evidence of the early Christians singing 2 Timothy 2:11-13, but we can easily imagine this scenario as the poetic features of the lines are evident. In the end, though, I don't think it matters what we call it. Instead of calling it a hymn, N.T. Wright has a different name for the passage: "Paul passes on to Timothy an early Christian proverb. It's the sort of thing you can imagine people learning by heart, teaching to their children and friends, and then repeating under their breath when standing before tribunals, when being threatened by angry magistrates or beaten by guards, when facing sudden and fierce temptation."[12] However we choose to name these verses, what is most significant is that these lines likely reflect a tradition that existed in the earliest church, one that Paul invokes here for his own purposes. As Mark Yarbrough says, "Tradition's purpose is perpetuation, and the power of human language, both written and oral, is arguably at is strongest when packaged in memorable production."[13]

Let's take a look first at one of the most famous and earliest creedal formulas in the New Testament, 1 Corinthians 15:3b-5. We'll follow that with a sampling of a few in the Pastoral Letters.

> *For I passed on to you as most important*
> *what I also received:*
> *that Christ died for our sins*
> *according to the Scriptures,*
> *that He was buried,*
> *that He was raised on the third day*
> *according to the Scriptures,*
> *and that He appeared to Cephas,*
> *then to the Twelve.*

This statement addresses matters that are "most important," ones that Paul both "received" and then "passed on." The passage meets one of the criteria for creedal formulae in that it is also chock-full of rare terms and expressions that Paul doesn't use anywhere else.[14]

The Pastoral Epistles, in particular, have a reputation for a high concentration of traditions such as creedal formulas and hymns.[15] Mark M. Yarbrough estimates that roughly one-fifth of 1 Timothy, is composed of preformed traditions.[16] Let's look at a few of those. In 1 Timothy 3:16, Paul sums up the mystery of Christian religion with beautiful poetic lines, using what most scholars think is a fragment of a hymn:

> *And most certainly, the mystery of godliness*
> *is great:*
> *He was manifested in the flesh,*
> *vindicated in the Spirit,*
> *seen by angels,*
> *preached among the nations,*
> *believed on in the world,*
> *taken up in glory.*

Also, check out 1 Timothy 6:13-14, which some suspect may have been a creedal formula used to prepare new converts for baptism:[17]

In the presence of God, who gives life to all, and of Christ Jesus, who gave a good confession before Pontius Pilate, I charge you to keep the command without fault or failure until the appearing of our Lord Jesus Christ.

And, let us not forget Titus, the last of our Pastoral letters. Titus 3:4-7 is a glorious text exalting the kindness of God. Some think it was possibly a baptismal hymn because of the allusion in verse 5:

> *But when the kindness of God our Savior and*
> *His love*
> *for mankind appeared,*
> *He saved us—*
> *not by works of righteousness that we had done,*
> *but according to His mercy,*
> *through the washing of regeneration*
> *and renewal by the Holy Spirit.*
> *He poured out this Spirit on us abundantly*
> *through Jesus Christ our Savior,*
> *so that having been justified by His grace,*
> *we may become heirs with the hope of*
> *eternal life.*

The other day I tweeted these lines: "grace has brought me safe thus far / and grace will lead me home."[18] You're totally humming it out loud right now, aren't you? Although not every Christian would recognize these lines, many would. And though the famous hymn has undergone many changes, the tradition itself has been a part of the Christian hymnal for hundreds of years. Identifying traditions such as hymns and creedal fragments in the New Testament, while tedious to some and intriguing for nerds like me, shows us something important. Paul wasn't an island. Even the great apostle knew he was a part of something a whole lot bigger than himself. In using these various traditions, Paul aligned himself with— joined his voice to—the common confessions of the earliest church.

Day Five

CAUGHT ALIVE

FLASH FORWARD: *But reject foolish and ignorant disputes, knowing that they breed quarrels.* **2 Timothy 2:23**

We learn how to fight. We don't have to learn how to cry, pout, or throw a tantrum. Those things come naturally to us. But as surely as a boxer is trained to knock out his opponent, we are trained by our early influencers how to fight. For example, I know and love a family of screamers. They live by the philosophy, *why say softly what you can yell?* It was the parents' way. It became the children's way and now the children's children have come of age and you guessed it—it's their way, too. Family time is a free-for-all fit for the set of a daytime talk show. Perhaps it's not entirely shocking that several members of the family haven't spoken to one another in years.

This commentary is admittedly coming from a shaky source. I have engaged in no few verbal scrapes. We Moores aren't the poster family for, well, *anything* except the grace of God. To say that conflict was no stranger to our home is like saying heat is no stranger to Houston. We are strong-willed and opinionated and have offended each other countless times. However, to the credit of Jesus alone, we are thicker than thieves and our fiercest words are usually steered toward one another's defense.

As compelling as discussing fighting strategies within our families can be, those of God's household will be on our docket today.

> **PLEASE READ 2 TIMOTHY 2:23-26 AND WRITE THE SEGMENT ON THE APPROPRIATE PAGE.**
>
> Describe Paul's insistent strategy for dealing with controversy and opposition. Be kind; not resentful, gently instruct

Social media is the mother lode for amateur sociologists. That's part of what I like about it. It's humanities in a snow globe. The world shakes and we stare through the glass dome to watch the flakes land. One person's musings may be mildly entertaining but nothing is like watching people relate, debate, congratulate, and hate one another with the theatrical flair that comes with public air. Depending on how much we indulge, we have live stream access to constant online courses in *how to have a fight*. Impressionable by nature, students can pick up the techniques of their favorite teachers at warp speed. Instead of pupils, we become parrots. Whom they hate, we hate. Whom they love, we love. Their name-dropping becomes our name-dropping and their name-calling becomes our name-calling. Mimicking takes the place of studying, and, instead of doing the independent work to draw informed conclusions, we perfect our impersonations.

As surely as parents tutor their children in conflict strategies, older Christians teach younger Christians how to handle opponents. If leaders they admire wield weapons of slander, followers will quick-draw the same. Have you ever wondered how we Christians get away with some of the things we do? We rename the sin something noble. We call gossip *informing*, judgment *discernment*, misogyny *authority*, anger *righteous indignation*, lust *appreciation*, arrogance *confidence*, profanity *passion*, and hate *debate*, and, voilà, misconduct gets reframed as *Christian duty*.

Every Christian is gifted for influence. We're all holding class whether or not we are intentional. In life and online, we are actively teaching how to speak, love, relate, fight, hate, encourage, discourage, build up, and tear down in the name of Jesus. Our overarching aim in this series is to become a mighty servant of God. Nothing brings our might to the light like the way we fight. You can take this one to the bank: gentleness with an opponent requires a lot more muscle than strong-arming a pair of giants.

Every Christian is gifted for influence.

LOOK BACK AT TODAY'S TEXT IN 2 TIMOTHY. How do you know Paul was not advocating silence as the godly response to error?

Gentle instruction to try + help them see truth (you need to know truth yourself first)

Earlier in the week we put a hold on 2 Timothy 2:14 so we could save it for today's similar context. What charge did Paul tell Timothy to issue?

Stop quarrelling it tears up the church

Consider this excerpt from New American Commentary:

The content of the warning includes an appeal to avoid "quarreling about words." This wrong emphasis can lead to aimless word splitting. "In the end disputing about words seeks not the victory of truth but the victory of the speaker." This word splitting involved useless verbal quibbling, but it did not focus on the aims of Christianity. Paul outlined two results of such verbal quibbles. First, it accomplishes no good purpose ("is useless," NASB; "is of no value," NIV). Second, it works to the ruin of those who participate in it ("brings destruction on those who hear it," Williams). The word for "ruins" (katastrophē) describes the tearing down of believers. It is the opposite of edification. Word splitting whets an appetite for argument rather than building commitment to the living God. In the heat of debate we must always ask ourselves if the subject is actually worth a fight and a searing disagreement.[9]

Fill in the blank according to the third sentence in the excerpt.
In the end disputing about words seeks not the
_____building up_____ but the __tearing down__ of believers

What is the Greek term that describes the tearing down of believers?
Katastrophé

What English word is obviously derived from that term?
Catastrophe

Intriguingly, the Greek word is used nowhere else in the entire New Testament.

CROSS REFERENCE 2 CORINTHIANS 13:10. **Toward what end had God given the apostle Paul authority?**
For _building you up_ and not _tearing you down_.

Sometimes we'll want in the worst way to sling mud with the best of them. We anticipate the adrenaline rush of feeling right, particularly if we're applauded by the right people. But we're called to keep it clean in the boxing ring even when our kindness is mistaken for weakness.

We'll spend our last few minutes on 2 Timothy 2:26, so please give it a fresh glance. Our abbreviated comments will not do this verse justice but we'll pick it up again in the video session following this lesson. In it, I'll share with you how I came face-to-face with the relevance of this verse on a frightening field trip rather than learning the lesson in the Bible classroom. I so want others to learn it in an easier way than I did.

Keeping Paul's terminology in verse 26 in mind, can you think of a time when you came to your senses? If so, what seemed to be the catalyst?

Over exaggerating & HS halts me—

The Greek meanings of two words in 2 Timothy 2:26 are particularly fascinating. The first one is translated "come to their senses."

Nepho — think of this like a small sin — we may eat d — take it like the seed & it traps us up

> ananēphō; from aná, again, and nēphō, to be sober. To awake out of a drunken sleep and become sober, to become sober (2 Tim. 2:26). This word may refer to a practice in which sowers scattered seeds impregnated with drugs intended to put birds to sleep that a net might be drawn over them to capture them.[10]

Here is an additional definition for further confirmation:

> ananepho (ἀνανήφω), "to return to soberness," as from a state of delirium or drunkenness (ana, "back," or "again," nepho, "to be sober, to be wary"), is used in 2 Tim. 2:26, "may recover themselves" (RV marg., "return to soberness," AV marg., "awake"), said of those who, opposing the truth through accepting perversions of it, fall into the snare of the Devil, becoming intoxicated with error; for these "recovery" is possible only by "repentance unto the knowledge of the truth."[11]

Are the definitions eye-opening in any way? If so, elaborate.

Yes see above

Do you think either definition suggests the person ensnared is not responsible for his/her error and sin? Support your answer here.

No we are responsible but w/o knew is solid truth thru study + having HS thru Grace — We walk right into the pit + even w/ those things we still do it sometimes

The second fascinating Greek word in 2 Timothy 2:26 is the one translated "captured." Read the definition, ignoring the blank. We will fill it in momentarily:

> zōgréō; from zōós, alive, and agreúō, to catch or entrap. To take alive, to catch, as hunters or fishermen do their game, hence applied spiritually to taking or catching men __by the preaching of the Gospel__. To take captive, used only spiritually for the captives of the devil in a moral sense, to ensnare, seduce (2 Tim. 2:26).[12]

In John 8:44, Jesus tells us that Satan "was a murderer from the beginning and has not stood in the truth, because there is no truth in him." Deception is Satan's murder weapon. Ultimately, he commits murder by deceiving people from believing in Jesus, robbing them of eternal life. Sometimes, however, the enemy has much to gain by capturing people alive. That's what the word *zogreo* means. Our word *zoo* evolved from it, drawing a vivid illustration of the concept.

> **List a few reasons why Satan's purposes could be well served by the exhibitions of lives he holds captive.** *If a church member - well respected - falls to sin - he becomes a stumbling block to so so many could be ~~be~~ saved people - ~~☒~~*

Boy, is that a discussion I wish we could have face-to-face. The devil is disturbingly powerful, methodical, and patient, draping a rope around his prey so loosely we don't realize it's there until our trapper jerks it tight. But make no mistake. Satan is no match for our God. If you are in Christ, "the One who is in you is greater than the one who is in the world" (1 John 4:4).

> **Psalm 18:3-19 is the most gorgeous account of deliverance from a snare that I know. Please read it—aloud if possible—as your conclusion to today's lesson.**

Oh, and about that fill-in-the-blank we left wide open. You didn't think I'd forgotten, did you? Go back to the definition of *zōgréō* and fill these words in the space: by the preaching of the gospel (Luke 5:10). A form of the exact same word *zōgréō* is used in Luke 5:10 when Jesus told a wide-eyed Simon Peter, "From now on you will be catching people!"

Try to absorb the glorious antithesis. Jesus catches people alive ...

... so they can live more abundantly.

... so they can be free from captivity.

... so they can love with intentionality.

Caught alive, so some of their suffering can be put to use this side of heaven and all of their suffering eclipsed by glory on the other.

Caught alive, so no casket can make a final claim on them.

Caught alive, so they can gallop thunderously across this dark globe carrying the light of the gospel like a torch of hope.

Group Session Four

INTRODUCTION

With your permission and patience, I'll share bits and pieces of my own story and Scriptures supporting their validity in hopes that a portion will be of value to you. The following are the five biggest eye-openers of my last forty years.

If you are in Christ, you are ___Called___.

THE FIVE EYE-OPENERS

1. The ___forces___ of ___evil___ are ___meaner___ and ___abler___ than most of us ___ever___ ___thought___.

   The more ___entangled___ we are, the less faithful we will be with what has been ___entrusted___ to us.

   - You are ___not___ ___your___ ___own___ ___worst___ ___enemy___.

   - But you are your ___own___ ___worst___ ___enemies___ best ___accomplice___.

   You can have a ___sincere___ and ___pure___ devotion to Christ and be ___seduced___ _____ by the devil.

2. This _faith life_ is a _fight_ from _beginning to end_ .

"_fight_" – Greek *"agōnízomai"* from *aghōn*, _conflict_ .
To _contend_ for _victory_ in the public games.
It generally came to mean to fight, wrestle. Figuratively, it is the task of faith in persevering amid temptation and opposition. It also came
to mean to _take_ _pains_ to wrestle as in
an _award_ _contest_ , straining every _mucles_ to
the _____ towards the _____ .

"_Good_" – Greek *kalos* – "_beautiful_ ; good"
harmonious – noble

3. Even amid the _evil_ that _beleagures_ or _befalls_ _us_ ,
God is continually and _mercifully_ after _our_ _good_ .

4. God purposely _put_ _up_ _the_ _system_
where it _demands_ _____ and _dependeny_
to _function_ _properly_

5. _Jesus_ _is_ _the_ _best_ _part_ .

WEEK FOUR

Difficult Times, Difficult People

Day One

IN THE LAST DAYS

FLASH FORWARD: *But know this: Difficult times will come in the last days.*
2 TIMOTHY 3:1

The world has gone mad and we with it. The fingertip of Adam or Eve could have carved those words in the blood-wet earth beside the body of their second child, murdered by their first. We think we've seen the world change in the course of our lifetimes but try to imagine what they experienced virtually overnight. What other mortal eyes have witnessed the world's deterioration with such immediacy? The first couple basked in a self-irrigating garden of fruit-bearing trees of untold tastes and varieties landscaped by the master Designer who communed with them. Earth's most magnificent sights—Australia's Great Barrier Reef, for instance, and its Rainbow Mountains in Zhangye Danxia—are like stray dust from Eden's winds compared to their native soil.

My writing desk at home (the one on the cover) sits at a picture window of a sunroom overlooking a small slope in our modest woods. Spring comes with sloppy kisses here, warm rains and sunshine coaxing every shade of green from limb and soil. A guest could be sorely tempted to throw off her shoes and run like a child on that cushiony grass down to our tiny pond. She'd get no further than twenty feet before the stinging nettles lent the distinct feeling she'd stepped in a bed of red ants. She would also need to back track and fetch my snake stick because she might meet the wrist-thick water moccasin I once found slithering on the edge of that sweet looking pond.

Just when we convince ourselves this world still bears faint images of Eden, a news alert of an earthquake pops up on the screens of our phones, tallying fatalities. This world is no paradise. Even if we could poison the thorns and pull up the thistles, planet Earth would still be treacherous ground because it is crawling with thorny people. If we combed through ancient literature, countless forms of the same basic question would surface: *What is this world coming to?* Check the context and we'd discover the catalyst to invariably be societal rather than circumstantial. It's also often generational. Few things are more predictable than an older generation feeling pretty certain the younger one will destroy the planet. Yet, here we are.

Do we, then, have grounds to call any part of what we're seeing in these current times *unprecedented*? We will grapple with that question throughout today and tomorrow's lessons.

PLEASE READ 2 TIMOTHY 3:1-5 AND WRITE IT IN THE BACK OF YOUR BOOK. This will serve as the handwritten portion for today and tomorrow.

Our primary focus today will be on dissecting and cross-referencing verse 1.

To begin, what time frame does Paul reference?

> *Last Days*

es•cha•tol•o•gy noun
plural -gies
[Greek *eschatos* last, farthest] 1844
1: a branch of theology concerned with the final events in the history of the world or of mankind
2: a belief concerning death, the end of the world, or the ultimate destiny of mankind specifically: any of various Christian doctrines concerning the Second Coming, the resurrection of the dead, or the Last Judgment.[1]

The Greek translated "in the last days" is *en eschatais hēmerais*. Circle the Greek word in the middle. If your pastor announces an upcoming sermon series on "eschatology" or you see a podcast or online course with that description, you can know the subject matter involves end-time events. Take a look at Merriam-Webster's definition of eschatology in the margin.

Biblical eschatology is fascinating, exhilarating, thrilling, chilling, and both hope and awe inspiring. Scholars similarly devoted to God and Scripture can differ dramatically in their interpretations of exact events involved, how the events will look, the order they will occur, which events are past tense and where the current generation fits on the time line. The inauguration of the era called "the last days" is easier to pin down.

Even if you've read Acts 2 a thousand times, please read it again from beginning to end, asking the Holy Spirit to make the words like fire in your bones. When you have finished reading, please complete the following:

What was the occasion (v. 1)? *Holy Spirit was poured out for the first time during Pentecost*

What was told to the gatherers in their own native languages (v. 11)?
> *The Gospel - the wonders of God*

REMEMBER PAUL'S SHORT-FORM GOSPEL IN 2 TIMOTHY 2:8? READ THE VERSE AGAIN. Do you see any similarity in Peter's gospel message in Acts 2:22-36? Briefly record the commonality.
> *Jesus raised from the dead - descended from David*

According to Acts 2:33, where was Jesus at the time Peter preached the sermon?
> *At in heaven*

According to the same verse, what had Jesus done resulting in what they were seeing and hearing?

poured out by the Holy Spirit

Write Acts 2:16 in the margin.

Fill in the following blank according to any major translation of Acts 2:17.

And it will be ___*In the last days*___ *God*, says God, that I will pour out My Spirit on all humanity; then your sons and your daughters will prophesy, your young men will see visions, and your old men will dream dreams.

2:16 No, this is what was spoken by the prophet Joel

There you have it. Under the unction of the Holy Spirit, Peter announced to the gatherers that "the last days" prophesied by the prophet Joel had officially begun. Dr. R. Earle voices a name for it:

> The expression "in the last days" (en eschatais hēmerais) comes from the OT (e.g., Isa 2:2; Mic 4:1). In Peter's quotation of Joel 2:28 on the day of Pentecost (Acts 2:17) it clearly refers to the whole messianic age, for he declared that the prophecy was being fulfilled that very day.[2]

For the sake of simplicity, let's round off to two thousand years and consider the implications. It seems that 730,485 is an inordinate number of days to assign to one era when we measure it against the average human lifespan but the timer is in the hands of the El Olam, the Eternal God. The clock started ticking with creation. "In the beginning God …" is the reference point for wrapping our minds around the terminology "in the last days … God …" This long-awaited era was nailed onto the time line at the crucifixion and it broke wide open when the stone rolled away from the tomb. Forty days later, Jesus ascended into the heavens to take His seat at God's right hand. Ten days later, timed to perfection on Israel's day of Pentecost, Jesus poured out the promised Holy Spirit in a spectacular exhibition followed by Peter's official public announcement. The era of "the last days" had officially broken in. That same glorious Spirit continues to spill on the life and in the heart of every individual—male or female—who receives the Messiah sent from God.

This overarching era called "the last days" will continue until what Paul termed "the day of Christ Jesus," a reference to Christ's return (Phil. 1:6). His second coming will usher in the final events of the original order. The apostle John, old and exiled on the island of Patmos, was the only disciple still drawing breath when Jesus revealed what would happen after the plan was fully accomplished.

Then I saw a new heaven and a new earth, for the first heaven and the first earth had passed away, and the sea no longer existed. I also saw the Holy City, new Jerusalem, coming down out of heaven from God, prepared like a bride adorned for her husband. Then I heard a loud voice from the throne: Look! God's dwelling is with humanity, and He will live with them. They will be His people, and God Himself will be with them and be their God. He will wipe away every tear from their eyes. Death will no longer exist; grief, crying, and pain will exist no longer, because the previous things have passed away. Then the One seated on the throne said, "Look! I am making everything new." He also said, "Write, because these words are faithful and true." And He said to me, "It is done! I am the Alpha and the Omega, the Beginning and the End. I will give water as a gift to the thirsty from the spring of life. and the Omega, the Beginning and the End.

REVELATION 21:1-6

READ REVELATION 21:1-6 IN THE MARGIN. What part of this promised future especially consoles or encourages you right now? Explain why.

It still baffles me—I am human so I'm not comforted by it—I love my family, I cling to them + know they are not followers so where will they be—it scares me.

The outstretched time line planned and penned by the master Designer goes stunningly full circle. The original "in the beginning" will come to its purposed end and God will call forth a new beginning that will never end. The beauty of it is almost unbearable. So why on the ever-loving earth does He wait? One last reading containing the phrase "in the last days" and we'll tie up the lesson.

READ 2 PETER 3:3-13. Is any portion of this segment new to you? If so, which one?

In your own words, explain the delay. *Waiting for everyone to hear the Gospel + choose—*

So here we find ourselves in these last days, jostled between the worst of times and best of times, the uprising of evil and the downpour of the Spirit. Christ's message echoes from the sacred page to each generation of servants: "Occupy till I come" (Luke 19:13, KJV). The world has gone mad but we don't have to go mad with it. We are the people of God, drenched by the Holy Spirit, defined by the Son of God, and dogged by a hoard of demons. We need God's wonders. We long for His wonders. We pray for His wonders. And I believe we will see many wonders. But one of the most grown-up realities we will ever accept is that we are His wonders with the greatest potential impact on the lost, the cynical, and the hopeless.

We—former liars, cheaters, idolaters, adulterers, mockers, haters, backstabbers, abusers, murderers, atheists, and narcissists—are placed by God right in the eyeshot of unbelievers who can refuse to look up but can't help looking out.

The Laying on of Hands, Part 1

My baby niece Willa was dedicated recently at church. To get the best view, I sat on the front row, my parents to my right and my nephew, Jackson, and oldest niece, Annabeth, to my left. At the end of the dedication we all stood up to say a collective prayer for this group of a dozen or so parents and babies.

Annabeth, seven, is my sidekick. She stood right in front of me pressed up against me, my arms draped around her neck. I took notice of her three-inch thick ponytail, identical to my sister's and mine. While we were standing, the campus pastor asked us to stretch out our hands as we prayed in agreement with him over the babies. Annabeth likes to be told what to do almost as much as I do, and so I smirked a bit when I felt her arms frozen stiff by her side. To my surprise, though, about midway through the prayer I saw her little hand pop up in the air.

For just a moment, time stood still.

My nieces and nephew are the closest things I have to kids of my own and the thought of them being caught up in the life of the church, its practices and rituals, overwhelmed me. The best way to describe what I felt is to say it was a sobering, weighty kind of gratefulness. It was not nostalgia.

I have never known life outside the church. I have known life in some tension with it here and there, but I've never one day known life outside it. I would have no concept of myself without the church. But let me tell you, growing up I tried to avoid the youth group and all its various functions to the best of my ability. I cringed my way through summer youth camp until I was old enough that the cute boys distracted me. I do not feel warmth in my heart about every experience I had growing up in the church. I feel awkward about some of it.

We have so many quirks, the church. We fail small and big and more often than we know or care to admit, but God is faithful to us and among us and despite us. Francis Spufford articulates the words of my heart more beautifully than I ever could:

"For us, you see, the church is not just another institution. It's a failing but never quite failed attempt, by limited people, to perpetuate the unlimited generosity of God in the world. ... That it exists, like Christ, in order to be a channel by which mending enters the world; a mending which, thank God, does not depend on the success of human virtue, individual or collective, but on what breathes and shines through us if we let it."[1]

For all its issues and faults, I'm grateful the church life is the life my nieces and nephew will get to live, too, even though I know it won't always be an easy one for them. They're pastor's kids and, as you know, a lot comes with being a pastor's kid. My prayer for them is that they will experience the beauty of the presence of God in the church like I did, for that alone changed everything about the course of my life. I hope they will grow up to one day have their own deep love for Scripture, worship, prayer, and even preaching.

The day of the baby dedication I was overcome by the children I love becoming participants in these practices so sacred to my heart.

While we were stretching out our hands in prayer I wondered what was going through Annabeth's mind. What did she think we were doing? And furthermore, what were we grown up Christians actually intending to accomplish by this act?

All these questions were swirling in my mind because as it happened, I was simultaneously studying the significance of the human hand and how in the Bible it often functions as a symbol of power. More specifically, I was doing research for this study on the gesture of laying hands on someone in the New Testament. I am referring to a religious act, one that frequently occurs during prayer. The "laying on of hands" is a gesture I've seen and experienced Christians doing my whole life. However, I have never heard any church leader talk about why we do it. When Mom and I started working on 2 Timothy I knew this was something I wanted to write about because of its significance in both 1 and 2 Timothy. We'll get to that in the next article, but for now, read Hebrews 6:1-2 a few times:

Therefore, leaving the elementary message about the Messiah, let us go on to maturity, not laying again the foundation of repentance from dead works, faith in God, teaching about ritual washings, laying on of hands, the resurrection of the dead, and eternal judgment.

The author of Hebrews rather surprisingly includes the laying on of hands among six things that make up the foundation of faith. Am I the only one who thinks that is wild? He exhorts his readers to now move beyond the basics but since many of us, including myself, are only just now seeing its significance, let's spend the next article investigating this part of the foundation.

Day Two

THE CHARACTER CRASH

FLASH FORWARD: *For people will be lovers of self, lovers of money, boastful, proud, blasphemers, disobedient to parents, ungrateful, unholy.* **2 TIMOTHY 3:2**

"Stop again, Buddy, and I'm going to have this baby in the car." I'd awakened before dawn that Sunday morning with intense abdominal pressure. One week earlier, my OB-GYN informed me that, based on recent test results, we were off on the due date by a month and I would not be full term for another three weeks. He may as well have said, "You have the gestation of an elephant. You should only be pregnant another year or so." I'd been told I'd need surgery to conceive. The diagnosis was terribly disappointing but not entirely out of left field. I'd inherited the condition from my mother and she'd dealt with infertility for nine years. Keith and I had been married nine and a half months.

Nothing is close in Houston, particularly when you're in labor. At the ten-minute mark of our twenty-five minute hospital trek, I'd rethought whether running by the church to teach my sixth grade Sunday School class had been judicious. Fifteen minutes in, I suggested Keith pick up speed. Twenty minutes in, I started threatening bodily harm if he slowed down at a traffic light again. By the time we pulled up to the hospital, I was red-faced and panting wildly.

I rushed into labor and delivery, threw on a hospital gown and was checked for progress. The nurse looked up at me deadpan. "Mrs. Moore, you are two centimeters dilated." It was the longest day of my life.

PLEASE READ MATTHEW 24:1-14. List the signs Jesus gave His disciples for His coming and the close of the age. *Cities destroyed, false Messiahs, wars, nation against nation, famine, earthquakes, persecution, death.*

What vivid imagery did Jesus use to describe the process in Matthew 24:8?
birth pains

What do you think that means?
it is a process — not all at once — not comfortable

How does Romans 8:22-25 convey something similar?
pain of childbirth

Keep those verses laboring in the background while we bring our text in 2 Timothy 3 to the foreground. Verses 2-4 contain eighteen descriptions promised to be prevalent enough in the last days to characterize humanity. Let's use an illustration to help us process the inundation of negative sociological influences.

Let the C's below represent Christians. Jot all 18 characteristics around and between the C's. In the blank at the bottom, fill in the 19th characteristic recorded in 2 Timothy 3:5.

③ C lovers of themselves - think of selfies   ① C lovers of money

C proud

C boastful   ③ C without self control   ① C abusive   ② C disobedient

② slanderous   unforgiving

② conceited   C unholy

C ungratful   ② brutal   C without love not lovers of the good

treacherous   ① rash   C Lovers of pleasure rather than lovers of God

2 TIMOTHY 3:5 Lovers of Pleasure rather than the lovers of God
Having a form of Godliness but denying its power

How does the 19th characteristic add a layer of complication?

We need to be careful that this does not happen to us - it is easy to be a fan it's worth sacrifice to be a follower

In yesterday and today's lessons, we're hovering over this question: Do we have grounds to call any of the characteristics we're seeing in these current times *unprecedented*? The globe bears the pocks and scars of thousands of years of natural disasters. Nearly 1950 years later, Mount Vesuvius still puffs out its chest like an arrogant Goliath over the ruins of Pompeii. The Antioch earthquake in A.D. 526 shook and silted the port of Seleucia Pieria, sifting the sand of some 250,000 inhabitants. As for man's contribution, history could talk itself hoarse recounting the host of human evils. The irony is that, second only to the question, *what's this world coming to?* may well be the question, *what's new under the sun?*

SOLOMON FELT THE ANGST AND OPPRESSION OF THE LATTER WHEN HE WROTE ECCLESIASTES 1:9. Write the verse in this space.

what has been done will be again,
what has been done will be done again;
this is nothing new under the sun

Those words were inscribed in the 10th century B.C. Doesn't the verse have a ring of familiarity regarding something we read in yesterday's lesson? Remember what Peter predicted the scoffers in the last days would say concerning the second advent of Christ?

> Where is the promise of His coming? Ever since the fathers fell asleep, all things continue as they have been since the beginning of creation.
> **2 PETER 3:4**

So, how do we reconcile two competing sociological questions in one era: the horrors of *what's this world coming to?* and the shoulder-shrugging *what's new under the sun?* Birth pains, that's how. Birth pains are driven by two involuntary forces: frequency and intensity. These forces are easiest to experience under the influence of an epidural, which might explain the overwhelming temptation to anesthetize with substance, sex, and social media in these deeply disturbing times. Not one characteristic on the 2 Timothy 3 list needs to be brand new to qualify for an end-time event. All it must do is intensify and accelerate. What's more, the comparison to birth pains brilliantly frees it from the demands of end-time enthusiasts for a fixed pattern of forward motion.

I'm writing this lesson within a year of my firstborn giving birth to her third-born. Melissa and I stood over Amanda for several hours of labor before leaving her and Curtis to welcome their little one. We watched the needle on the monitor for every peak and calculated the precise minutes and seconds in between. Even though she was progressing toward delivery, her contractions did not always advance at a predictable pace. "That last one was pretty big," I'd say. "This next one is liable to be huge." Sometimes, however, the next contraction was weaker, making us wonder if her labor was digressing. It wasn't. By the final hour the contractions were coming like a freight train barely slowing down at a crossing.

The characteristics listed in 2 Timothy 3:2-5 are not any newer to the world scene than earthquakes, famines, lawlessness, cold-heartedness, betrayal, and religious persecution. The newness will be the prevalence, occurrence burgeoning into prominence. Formerly localized social malignancies will spread into invasive cancers. The invasiveness can indeed qualify as *unprecedented.*

Go back to the illustration with the C's and shove aside your inner over-reactor and approach it like a cool-headed researcher. Underline each characteristic you would conservatively estimate as having notably increased. Now write a 1, 2, or 3 beside each characteristic you underlined to estimate the level of increase in the last decade. (1 = notable; 2 = eye-opening; 3 = jarring) Finally, pick two of the characteristics you assigned a "3," write them in the blanks below and, underneath, support each estimate with several examples.

brutal

think of online decapitations or drownings — crazy

lovers of self

selfies — social media — pampering — I deserve to be this or that —

without self control

Everyone wants everything + right now — digital media helps perpetuate that —

You don't need to know a single letter of the Greek alphabet to appreciate this excerpt from G. W. Knight's commentary on the descriptions in 2 Timothy 3:2-5.

The list has a somewhat chiastic arrangement: It begins and ends with terms expressing similar concepts and has within this framework other matched groupings of terms working from the beginning and end of the list:

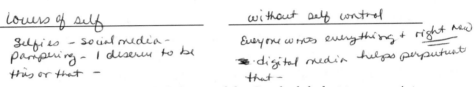

φίλαυτοι [lovers of self]

φιλάργυροι [lovers of money]

ἀλαζόνες [boastful]

ὑπερήφανοι [proud]

βλάσφημοι [blasphemers]

  γονεῦσιν ἀπειθεῖς [disobedient to parents]

  ἀχάριστοι [ungrateful]

  ἀνόσιοι [unholy]

  ἄστοργοι [unloving]

  ἄσπονδοι [irreconcilable]

    διάβολοι [slanderers]

  ἀκρατεῖς [without self-control]

  ἀνήμεροι [brutal]

  ἀφιλάγαθοι [without love for what is good]

προδόται [traitors]

προπετεῖς [reckless]

τετυφωμένοι [conceited]

φιλήδονοι [lovers of pleasure]

μᾶλλον ἤ φιλόθεοι [rather than lovers of God]

The list begins and ends with words expressing a misdirection of "love."
This suggests that what is fundamentally wrong with these people
is that their life is misdirected and that the other vices flow from this
misdirection.[2]

All it takes to appreciate the arrangement is noting the repetition of the first
letter in several word groups. For example, note the eight words in the middle
beginning with *ά*. Star each of them. These are *ά*-privative words (also called
alpha-privative).

In each case the ά- negates some good quality, so that this group of words
describes these people as not manifesting even the basic characteristics
of human life that God's common grace usually affords.[3]

The *ά* (the equivalent of our "a" in English) prefix negates the term. The word
atheist is a perfect example. The prefix "a" conveys lack of belief in God (or a
god). All eight of the *ά*-privative Greek words Paul employed express what
individuals entirely given over to self-worship *lack*. Consider how many people
reject God because they are convinced He's a taker instead of a giver. The twist
is that the surest equation for a life of subtraction is self-exaltation. The more
we give self, the less self gets. In our translations of 2 Timothy 3:2-3, the Greek
ά-privatives are most obvious in the words with our English prefix "un."

Ungrateful: lacking _gratefullness_.

Unholy: lacking _holiness_.

The second characteristic in verse 3 is worth particular pause. The HCSB
translates the Greek *aspondoi* "irreconcilable." It means *lacking the willingness*
or desire to _recconcile_. Imagine societies populated by greater
and greater numbers of individuals who are less and less willing to reconcile.
Think even broader than marriages. Consider friendships, siblings, business
partnerships, and lawsuits.

Have you ever deeply desired reconciliation and been refused?
Describe what you felt. frustrated + sad   — missy

What would be the ramifications of an entire culture marked by an
unwillingness to reconcile? ugliness, fighting, bitterness, not being
social so lonely

Go back to the list of Greek words in Dr. Knight's excerpt. Circle the first two words that begin with φ (translated ph in English) then look at the last two lines. Circle the two words beginning with the same letter. Draw an arrow from the top set to the bottom set. Reread Dr. Knight's summation and fill in these blanks.

The list begins and ends with words expressing a
~~tota~~ misdirection of love . This suggests that what
is _fundamentally_ _wrong_ with these people is
that their life is misdirected and that the _other vices_
flow from this misdirection.

How would you summarize Dr. Knight's conclusion?
Sounds reasonable — ~~when~~ when we are self centered we
miss everyone else —

The two bookends support every item on the shelf. Put another way they are the parents of the malevolent offspring between them.

The list begins with "lovers of _~~self~~ self_ " in verse 2 and
ends in verse 4 with "lovers of _~~self~~ pleasure_ rather than
lovers of God."

Cut to the heart of the list and one of the most disturbing characteristics will bleed to the surface.

What word does your Bible translation supply at the very beginning of
verse 3? _Lovers of self_

Several translations use the word *unloving*. The KJV probably translates it best: "without natural affection." The Greek word *ástorgos* is comprised of "the privative *á*, without, and the noun *storgē*, family love. Without family love (Rom. 1:31; 2 Tim. 3:3)." The word doesn't mean generally unloving. It conveys a widespread fraying of the most fundamental ties. Husband and wife. Parent and child. Brother and sister. Grandparent and grandchild.

Whether or not these are the last days of the last days, these are our last days. Our mortal lives are a flash in the pan. The world that surrounds us is the world God assigned us. Glance back at the C's illustration on page 120 one more time. The church of the present—comprised of every Christian on planet Earth—has a rock-solid foundation but it doesn't have walls. It's not meant to. It is made up of porous skin. We will have to labor hard and break a sweat sometimes to keep from absorbing the brutality of a culture in love with itself.

Day Three

STRONG-WILLED WOMEN

FLASH FORWARD: *For among them are those who creep into households and capture weak women, burdened with sins and led astray by various passions.*
2 TIMOTHY 3:6, ESV

Gear up because we are about to take care of some business. Let this be a red-letter day on our calendars when we made up our minds about who we weren't going to be. We didn't get to choose our DNA. We didn't get to choose our body type. We didn't get to choose our birthday or our time slot in history. We didn't even choose many of our circumstances and challenges. But make no mistake, we do get to choose what kind of people we're going to be. We are not helpless victims to our natural bents. Our weak pasts don't get to strong-arm our futures. Our unmet needs don't have to be the breeding grounds of our defeat. Let this be the day when we looked ourselves squarely in the mirror and said, "I don't know exactly who you're going to turn out to be but I know who you're not."

PLEASE READ 2 TIMOTHY 3:6-9 AND HANDWRITE IT IN THE BACK OF YOUR WORKBOOK.

You probably aren't left to wonder which two verses are elevating the temperature of the lesson today. The wording in the NET is particularly chromatic:

> For some of these insinuate themselves into households and captivate weak women who are overwhelmed with sins and led along by various passions. Such women are always seeking instruction, yet never able to arrive at a knowledge of the truth.
> 2 TIMOTHY 3:6-7, NET

The adjective used by the NIV84 has stuck with me and made me squirm for years: *weak-willed women*. Sometimes the Word of God has to offend our sensibilities to defend our honor. Let's get two facts lined out quickly so we don't get defensive.

Don't be information rich & application poor

Cheryl: *What is your grander vision for women you teach?*

Beth: *I can answer this one in a heartbeat! I want each woman to know to the marrow of her bones she is audaciously loved by Jesus Christ and to audaciously love Him back. This divine love drives all else of greatest value. If we boldly love Jesus, we will boldly seek Him, boldly serve Him, boldly obey Him, boldly trust Him, boldly share Him, boldly endure in Him through hardship and suffering, and boldly forgive when we're offended. Big bold love. That's what I want for every woman. And man.*

1. **PAUL WAS NOT PICKING ON WOMEN.** Keep in mind that every exhortation in the entire letter was addressed to a man and every name Paul called out in a negative context or with a spiritual indictment belonged to a male. Anyone who can get to the end of 1 and 2 Timothy and claim Paul took it easy on men isn't paying attention.

2. **PAUL WAS NOT DESCRIBING ALL WOMEN.** He was describing the kind most vulnerable to deception and to slick, sly manipulators.

Maybe you have never been one of them. But I have. Not all slick, sly manipulators are men and not all weak-willed individuals led along by various passions are women. In the immediate context, Paul was almost certainly describing false teachers in Ephesus who'd ensnared many females.

Sometimes weak-willed people are easy to spot. Other times they are harder to peg because their weak wills are selective. In my case, I was strong-willed in numerous areas. To God's gracious credit alone, I was goal-oriented, self-disciplined, and value-driven. When I made up my mind about something, I usually followed through. But, in matters revolving around sexuality, I continuously caved under pressure and made incredibly foolish decisions. Sexual sin crept through the cracks of my home like poison ivy and probably choked off the development of much needed boundaries, but who knows? I might have made similar decisions anyway. The infamous sexual revolution was already well under way when I came of age. I made numerous mistakes and misjudgments in other areas also. They simply weren't as consistent. Let's not be quick to restrict the kinds of things that can lasso weak-willed people into deception and sin. In the wording of the HCSB, these individuals are "led along by a variety of passions."

Passions are cravings, longings, and desires that beg to be indulged. Perhaps like me you've been frustratingly weak-willed in some areas more than others.

If you're willing, express those here in order to bring them into the light (Eph. 5:13-14). You won't be asked to share these with your small group.

Def. I needed the approval of men — at any cost — no identity. — Sensory satisfaction also like food —

The gratification of caving to the craving drops in like a sanguine friend but it never sits down and makes itself at home. It squeals out of the driveway just in time for the clunkers of guilt and failure to lumber up to the curb and unload a months-worth of baggage. Their invasion was the devil's plan when he dispatched the temptation. He, too, is destination-oriented like his divine nemesis but his compass lacks a North. His destination of choice for us is, of course, hell, but, if our heavenly course is already set, he'll settle for steering us into a ditch. He wants us too defeated to disturb the darkness. ———————— *too defeated to lead others to the gate*

Focus on the HCSB translation again: (led along) by a variety of *passions.* Circle the first two words.

Passions are drivers. By their very nature, they take us somewhere. On any given day, something is driving us. Imagine the variety of emotions and mind-sets that can elbow their way to the wheel and steer us. Selfish ambition runs-over people. Jealousy side-swipes the cars in other lanes. Bitterness shifts into reverse and backs over people. Gluttony keeps circling the drive-thru. Narcissism drives like no one else is on the road. Procrastination keeps its blinker on but never makes the turn. Seduction drives while intoxicated. Rage throws a match in the gas tank. Despair only takes tunnels.

Lack of self control - texts while driving on the expressway

Low of self - sees the rearview mirror facing them instead of the back window)

Can you think of an additional word picture?

One more and it's not an emotion or mind-set. It is a divinely designed dimension of our humanity. Sexuality is a God-intended passenger in our personal journey but it is a terrible driver. It will not steer us where we want to go. It will drive us into ditch after ditch and, if we don't shove it away from the wheel, will leave us engulfed in mud like quicksand.

How about some good news waving like a banner on the horizon? Forms of the Greek word *epithumiais* translated *passions* in 2 Timothy 3:6 are also found in positive, sacred contexts.

Look up each verse and record the nature of the deep desire and who possessed it:

PHILIPPIANS 1:23 *desire to move on - leave problems behind*

1 THESSALONIANS 2:17 *desire to see those we love*

LUKE 22:15 *desire to meet up w/ loved ones again*

God does not advocate the death of desire. He advocates healthy desire. Take the pulse of Psalm 63 if you need proof. If that's not passion, it can't be found on the page. Embracing this concept shifts the atmosphere for me. I was born with a white-hot heart. I don't want to be want-less. The newsflash is that God doesn't want that either. He's not shutting down our passions. He's reframing our hearts for passions that won't burn them to a black crisp. When God revealed Himself to Moses in the burning bush in Exodus 3:2, what drew Moses to the sight was the anomaly of a fire that didn't destroy the bush. That is godly passion. Our hearts burning without charring and scarring.

In our vocabulary, the description *strong-willed* is synonymous with obstinate and rebellious. If, for instance, I told you I had a strong-willed four-year old, what might you say?

he is stubborn

> No one becomes a mighty servant of God without becoming strong willed about God's will.

We get to challenge that strictly negative connotation in today's lesson. No one becomes a mighty servant of God without becoming strong willed about God's will. Characteristics like submissiveness, gentleness, meekness, and humility are not signs of weakness. They push back hard against the immense force of our human natures. They are burly witnesses flexing their muscles, strong willed about God's will. In several Scriptures, weakness is viewed nobly. However, being weak and being weak willed are very different things.

How would you explain the difference between them?

weak is not strong
weak willed is easily moved to different ideas – James 1:6
tossed about like waves

If we're going to stay faithful to God and endure in times of weakness, we need a strong will about God's will. By no weak will did Rahab the prostitute hide the Hebrew spies. By no weak will did Joshua march an army around the walls of Jericho. By no weak will did Daniel resolve not to defile himself with Nebuchadnezzar's delicacies. By no weak will did David refuse to avenge himself against a maniacal Saul. By no weak will did Esther dare to seek audience with the king for the lives of her people. By no weak will did James and John rock their father's boat and pitch their nets so they could follow Jesus. Thousands upon thousands haven't sacrificed their lives rather than renounce Jesus Christ out of a weak will. It takes being strong willed about God's will to be obedient and fulfill our callings. When your life is done, let the record show: By no weak will did _____*Rcarmoner*_____ ... *chose to be*
a Christian

Nothing is cute about a weak-willed woman ruled by her natural passions. She may attract the attention of opportunists but she can't keep their interest without their respect. Her weakness will not cause her to be loved. It will cause her to be used. She can seek instruction until her brain fries but her bondage has quashed her discernment and left her gullible. Her feet are drawn to a road of deception that cannot deliver her to a destination of truth. Until she opens her eyes and repents. Thank God.

Think of the women — by the well — man after man + still unloved but well used.

Think of Samson — weak-willed + easily used.

I have a feeling some part of this discussion is hitting a nerve, whether in regard to your own journey or another you witnessed. If you're willing, share your story.

pajamas stolen - looking for acceptance

Go back and read 2 Timothy 3:6-9 again. Beware of instant intimacy, of relationships that go from zero to one hundred overnight. Healthy relationships take time. They respect boundaries. Beware of people who may be affable and helpful but start invading every artery of your life. Beware of individuals you have trouble saying no to. Be cautious about anyone who gets offended when you're the least bit out of touch or jealous when you're not together. Beware of anyone who starts coming between you and your spouse or you and your family, your other time-tested friends or godly commitments. Stop dead in your tracks over *anyone* who wants to be your *only one*. Even a prospective mate who increasingly isolates you should cause you to raise your eyebrows. Inordinate possessiveness and oppressiveness love to double date. You may be flattered at first but flattery quickly turns into misery. Are you getting an internal red flag? Heed it even before you can explain it.

Some of the world's best emotional predators masquerade with neediness. They will insinuate themselves into your household through the underground pipes of your sympathies. Bottom line: anyone who feeds your weak will about God's will can wreak hellacious havoc.

Guard your heart. Guard your home. Guard your body. These shields interlock to guard your calling.

We get to make a decision today. We get to decide who we're not going to be.

Day Four

BUT AS FOR YOU

FLASH FORWARD: *But you have followed my teaching, conduct, purpose, faith, patience, love, and endurance.* 2 TIMOTHY 3:10

If rubber had been invented in the first century, I feel like the saying "this is where the rubber meets the road" might have made it into Paul's last letter to Timothy. It's a shame he couldn't have written it prophetically. Just think how the apostle Paul could have used this idiom in his response to critics: "I'm rubber; you're glue. Whatever you say bounces off of me and sticks to you."

Paul's tone in 2 Timothy spikes to peak decibels in the opening verses of chapter 3. Every godless description of people in the last days hits the page like a foot stomping on the pedal of a kick drum. Read the portion again and, this time, turn up the volume and imagine that rubber beater pounding a drum.

> ... lovers of self, lovers of money, boastful, proud, blasphemers, disobedient to parents, ungrateful, unholy, unloving, irreconcilable, slanderers, without self-control, brutal, without love for what is good, traitors, reckless, conceited, lovers of pleasure rather than lovers of God, holding to the form of godliness but denying its power.
> 2 TIMOTHY 3:2-5

"This is what people surrounding you will increasingly be like," the apostle told his beloved son in the faith. And then Paul wrote two words that changed the entire trajectory. Two words that defy demons. Two words powerful enough to push back the pressures of an entire populace. Two words that evaporate excuses. Two words that halt all the finger pointing. Two words that keep us from thinking someone else's faithfulness counts as ours.

But you.

AND THOSE TWO WORDS ARE WHERE THE RUBBER MEETS THE ROAD. Please read 2 Timothy 3:10-13 and write the segment in the back of the book.

Paul is long gone. Timothy's no longer here. *But you ...*

Those are two of the most defiant words you may come across in the wide stretch of this Bible study journey. This pair could become the response that begs to differ with a mile-long list of limiting assumptions and obstacles. A dozen examples:

All sorts of odds are stacked against me. *But you ...*

None of my friends are this serious about Jesus. *But you ...*

I don't have a Bible degree. *But you ...* .

I come from a terrible background. *But you ...* .

My family members are all agnostics. *But you ...*

My work environment is oppressive and godless. *But you ...*

I have children with special needs. (Or, I have special needs.) *But you ...*

I wanted to get married first so I could serve with a spouse. *But you ...*

I'm just in high school. (Or, I'm already in my eighties.) *But you ...*

I committed a felony. *But you ...*

I'm way too busy. *But you ...*

I'm not great at this kind of stuff. *But you ...*

Write two more statements that are pertinent to you and follow them up with those two defiant words:

1. I'm always so busy. But you...

2. I have responsibilities here.. but you

List the nine dimensions of Paul's life Timothy had followed (vv. 10-11).

purpose, faith, patience, love, endurance, persecutions, suffering, way of life,

Most of us want to follow the love and faith of those we esteem in Christ, but who on earth is crazy enough to sign up for their persecutions and sufferings? The paradox is this: if we never need rescuing, we'll never know the Rescuer. Something happens in a divine rescue that you can't simulate in a classroom—something you can't experience through someone else's story. The unseen Defender comes to your defense. And He comes for you. It is personal. And shameless. Jesus can't sweep you up in His arms and carry you out of harsh conditions that never had you cornered. Paul and Silas would have missed the quake that broke their chains had they missed the jail that held them. Had their backs not been lashed, they might have slept right through those midnight songs. Psalm 116 bursts on the page with the opening words "I love the LORD because ..." Not coincidentally, the psalm is a testament to divine rescue. Show me someone who deeply loves the Lord and I'll show you someone who has known His rescue. In the visible realm, there may be love at first sight but, with an unseen Rescuer, it's often love at first flight.

The paradox is this: if we never need rescuing, we'll never know the Rescuer.

Paul's relentless faithfulness to Jesus would have been a hard act to follow. His second and final letter to Timothy was his way of saying, "You have what it takes. Put it to use."

Humor me with the interjection of a story I keep getting tickled over. Before becoming familiar with a journalist who writes Christian news satire, I happened on a breaking-news article reporting that a well-known and deeply respected pastor had, in his great passion for God, gestured so wildly in a sermon that he accidentally punched himself in the mouth. According to the article, he spit several teeth into his palm and continued boldly preaching, bloodied and undaunted. I wouldn't have been so gullible had I been less familiar. I know the pastor and, if anyone on the earth is dedicated and humble enough to preach the Scriptures after knocking out two teeth, in my estimation, it would be him.

Now for the most pathetic part. For a split second my heart sunk, surmising that, while I do indeed have what it takes to accidentally punch myself in the face while gesturing wildly, I do not likely have what it takes to spit my teeth into my palm and teach the remainder of a lesson. Later that night at family supper, I mentioned to my daughters and son-in-law how sorry I felt for the pastor, how he was owed more respect than that and how it was a wonder I'd not at least given myself a black eye. After staring at me in disbelief, all three of them leaned forward, elbows on the table, and exclaimed, "Mom! It wasn't true!" We laughed until we cried.

Staunch servants of Christ have come before us. Some in the first century. Some in the last century. We hear about them and marvel over what they were able to accomplish and endure. Their faithfulness to Jesus seems a hard act to follow, but, the truth is, we have what it takes. We either already possess it or have complete access to it because we have God's own Holy Spirit and His Word. The red carpet is rolled out in front of us. It is the way of the cross, yes. But is it also the way of "the King eternal, immortal, invisible, the only God" (1 Tim. 1:17). The One who "always leads us in triumphal procession, and through us spreads the fragrance of the knowledge of him everywhere" (2 Cor. 2:14, ESV). Jesus has been setting you up for years to be a mighty servant. You may reply, "You have no idea how disastrous my last years have been." But even the aspects and experiences in your life you've hated are bought back by His redemption and wrung to every last drop by Christ's scarred hands for your equipping. You have what it takes.

Jesus has been setting you up for years to be a mighty servant.

And, this, my friend, is where the rubber meets the road. This is where our study starts moving from our desks to our backpacks and from the page to the pavement. This is where we stop being mesmerized by Christian celebrity culture and have guts enough to fulfill our own callings. Maybe you've been so distracted by what others have to offer, you've overlooked what you have to give. Bless them, encourage them, gain from them, and enjoy them but get this through your head: You also have what it takes. You also have a wealth to offer. You are your own mix of gifts, skills, and experiences God wants to stir up to serve His Son.

How have you allowed the giftedness and serving lives of others to distract you from what you have to give? *I'm no Beth Moore, I'm no memorizer, strong preacher, I use other peoples words BC I am not quick enough to use my own.*

Take a quick evaluation. How has God shaped you to serve? *He made me bold + I'm a talker —*

You <u>have what</u> it takes.

If we get to the end of this study with a good look over our shoulder at the journeys of Paul and Timothy but no clear gaze ahead at the path we're called to walk with equal tenacity, we will have missed the mission in 2 Timothy's message. We—common people with common problems—get to carry on the uncommon legacies of Paul and Timothy. To do so deliberately will be to do so most effectively.

The diagram on page 135 most likely looks familiar. It is similar to the one we filled in on Day One of Week One with our biographical sketch of Paul. This time both the figures represent your own life. The cradle represents your birth and infancy. The upright figures represent you presently. Turn back to the diagram you filled out for Paul (page 18) and study it for several minutes, noting the nature of the information you recorded. While Paul's biographical sketch on Day One only extended to his young adulthood, yours is intended to reach your present age.

> In small print, please document the following pieces of autobiographical information in appropriate places on the diagram but leave the space underneath it as well as above the arrows blank until our next lesson. Please check each piece of information off as you go:
>
> _____ Record birthdate and birth place directly below the cradle. If anything was unusual about your birth, add that information.
>
> _____ Record today's date, your current age, and your current city directly below the figures on the right.
>
> _____ Place a cross between the cradle and the people to represent when you accepted Jesus as your Savior and write beside it the age you were at the time.
>
> _____ In the space between the cradle and the people, include abbreviations in chronological order to represent where you attended school, where you attended church if applicable, and the primary places you've worked. If those pieces of information are too numerous, include the ones most formative to you, whether in a negative or positive sense.
>
> _____ Lastly, please jot current biographical information below the upright figure. (This documentation might include information such as married or single, the name of your school, occupation or primary responsibility, where you attend church and connect with fellow believers, etc. Make the diagram yours. The purpose is to depict an overview of your autobiography.)

Thank you for your diligence! We will finish the diagram on Day Five. Life is too hard on this fallen planet to comprise an authentic autobiographical sketch without a single negative feeling. When your sketch is complete, any glaring absence of people, stability, or opportunity will only serve to dip the brush deeper in the paint to slather two bright words across your story:

But you ...!

I'm profoundly blessed to journey with you. Stay the course!

The Laying on of Hands, Part 2

In John Fleter Tipei's monograph The Laying On of Hands in the New Testament: Its Significance, Techniques, and Effects, he explains: "In the ancient world, the human hand was a universal symbol of power. It was looked upon as an instrument which actually conveys power from one person to another."[2]

In the NT the act of laying on hands is usually conveyed with a form of the Greek phrases: ἐπιτίθημι +ō χείρ or ἐπιτίθημι + ō χείρ.[3] The English translations vary but are often translated as "to lay hands" or "to place hands" or "(the) laying on of hands." In the New Testament, the phenomenon began during the ministry of Jesus and then developed in earliest Christianity as a formal gesture, one in which prayer was frequently involved.

The laying on of hands is used in association with four primary things:
1) Blessing
2) Healing
3) The Reception of the Holy Spirit
4) Commissioning/Ordination/ Assignment

The four categories do overlap some. For example, the idea of blessing is probably inherent in all four categories. Let's start there.

BLESSING. When Jesus lays His hands on a group of children in the Synoptic Gospel passages, the purpose seems primarily to be blessing (Matt. 19:13-15; Mark 10:13-16; Luke 18:15-17). As Tipei explains, "In placing His hands on children Jesus was blessing them; that is, the gesture was a 'symbol of a transfer of blessing' from Jesus to them. Its purpose was 'primarily to identify the person(s) who receives the blessing' and also to serve as 'a sign of Jesus' identification with and acceptance of this marginalized category of human beings."[4]

HEALING. In the Gospels, Jesus often lays hands on the people He heals (Mark 5:23; 6:5, 7:32; 8:22-26; Luke 4:40; 13:13), though it is not necessary since He is also able to heal by a mere word (Matt. 8:8-13; Mark 2:11). Likewise, followers of Jesus also lay hands on people and heal them, such as Ananias when he placed his hands on the light-blinded Paul in Damascus (Acts 9:12,17), then Paul himself when he healed the father of Publius on the island of Malta (Acts 28:8).

THE RECEPTION OF THE HOLY SPIRIT. There are three instances in Acts when the reception of the Holy Spirit is associated with the laying on of hands: the Samaritan converts, Paul's conversion in Damascus, and the Ephesians (Acts 8:17-18; 9:12,17; 19:6). One of these episodes involves a guy named Simon who had a reputation for dazzling people with black magic.

He believed in the name of Jesus and was baptized during the ministry of Philip in Samaria.

When the apostles in Jerusalem heard the news about the people in Samaria responding to the word of God, they sent Peter and John to check things out. When Peter and John arrived, they prayed for the new believers to receive the Holy Spirit, because the Holy Spirit had not yet come on any of them. Acts 8:17 says that Peter and John placed their hands on the believers, and they received the Holy Spirit. Simon then offered Peter and John money so that he too would have the power to lay hands on people and give them the gift of the Holy Spirit. The two apostles, however, called him to repent instead. This scene is wild! Simon knew something about captivating crowds. Whatever happened when the apostles laid hands on the new converts, it was clearly spectacular enough that he thought he could eventually capitalize on the ability to do it himself (Acts 8:18-24).

COMMISSIONING/ORDINATION/ ASSIGNMENT. The main idea in this last category is that through the laying on of hands a person is assigned to a given task and granted grace to carry out that assignment. Robert Wall, regarding the background of this particular function of laying on of hands, says, "Most locate it in the Diaspora synagogue where 'laying on of hands' was a liturgical gesture in the ordination of rabbis—not merely the transference of spiritual authority to those who qualified by a public recognition of that authority for a congregation to observe."[5] In Acts 6, the Twelve summon a body of disciples to select a group of seven men from among them who would function as the first deacons. After the seven were chosen for the task, the apostles prayed for them and laid hands on them (Acts 6:6). A second example, in Acts 13, occurs in the church of Antioch and is more akin to what we think of as a commissioning or a sending out. A group of prophets and teachers were worshiping and fasting and "the Holy Spirit said, 'Set apart for me Barnabas and Saul for the work to which I have called them'" (Acts 13:2). After fasting and praying, the group laid their hands on Barnabas and Saul and sent them off to Cyprus for mission work (v. 3).

This brings us to the Pastoral Epistles. As you recall from chapter 1 in 2 Timothy, Paul exhorts Timothy "to keep ablaze the gift of God that is in you through *the laying on of my hands*" (2 Tim. 1:6, emphasis mine). So also in 1 Timothy 4:14 Paul says: "Do not neglect the gift that is in you; it was given to you through prophecy, with *the laying on of hands* by the council of elders" (emphasis mine). Some interpreters think these two verses depict the same occasion while others suggest they depict two different occasions. The argument for two occurrences comes from the wording in the different passages. In 2 Timothy 1:6 it is Paul alone laying hands on Timothy, while in 1 Timothy 4:14 Paul states that a council of elders laid hands on the young man. We can't know for sure, but it's possible Paul was among the council of elders and only refers to himself in 2 Timothy due to the more personal nature of that letter. Paul also warns Timothy in an intriguing note at the end of the first letter not to lay hands on anyone hastily. Here he is probably referring to Timothy's own eventual ordination of future elders (1 Tim. 5:17-22).

But back to 2 Timothy 1:6:

I remind you to keep ablaze the gift of God that is in you through the laying on of my hands.

What "gift" is mediated by the laying on of hands? It could refer to an endowment for carrying out a task or the Holy Spirit. I prefer the former reading but there are plenty of scholars who think the gift is the Holy Spirit. What strikes me, though, no matter what the gift refers to, is that actual human hands like ours could be mediators of the divine gift. Now Timothy is subsequently responsible for this gift he possesses, for the text says he must rekindle it or keep it ablaze. But when we think of "gifts" we usually conceive of qualities that are inherent even if latent in us. We know that Timothy was an exceptional guy, commended by Christians not only in his own town but also in Iconium, a town approximately 18 miles away (Acts 16:2).[6]

In addition, Timothy had a divine gift that was not native to him; it was given to him by God.

Whether God used Paul's hands to transfer the gift or as a symbol of the delivery is unknown. Regardless, I'm moved by this because it shows us in an explicit way how dependent we are on each other to fulfill the tasks to which God has called us. In an individualistic "Jesus and me" culture, that instructs me.

GOD-BREATHED

FLASH FORWARD: *All Scripture is inspired by God and is profitable for teaching, for rebuking, for correcting, for training in righteousness, so that the man of God may be complete, equipped for every good work.* 2 TIMOTHY 3:16-17

Every now and then the majesty, enormity, and wonder of God hits us with such force our minds feel like they could explode. The catalyst could be something we've seen a hundred times but somehow a fresh profoundness washes over us. For example, I've heard the stories of Jesus' miracles since earliest childhood but not long ago the account of Jesus walking on water nearly took my breath away. He didn't bother parting the sea. He actually stepped right up on top of it and the waves became a floor under His feet. Wrap your mind around that.

Here's another mind-bender with a bearing on today's lesson: God created the universe—not out of thin air but out of absolutely nothing—*with His voice.* Keep reading that sentence until the overfamiliarity wears off. God said, "Let there be light," and there it was, like someone flipping on blinding lights in a stadium on a pitch-black night. God said, "Let the earth produce vegetation," and that it did. Instant sprouts. Full-grown trees, limbs drooping and dripping with fruit exotic enough to make a mango blush.

This is key: By His sovereign design, God did not create solely with sound. He could have, yet He didn't. He accompanied the sound with His breath. Mind you, God does not *need* to breathe. He is self-existent. He is not reliant on any element including air. He speaks and breathes according to His own will, and, by that same will, He ordained the two to work at times in tandem. Read Psalm 33:6-9 in the margin and fill in the following blanks according to the first sentence:

> The heavens were made by ___the word of the Lord___, and all the stars, by ___the breath of his mouth___.

God created humankind in His image, seeing fit that speech would not be a product solely of sound. He ordained breath to bring volume. Test the interconnectedness by attempting to read the segment from Psalm 33 while holding your breath.

> The heavens were made by the word of the LORD,
> and all the stars, by the breath of His mouth.
> He gathers the waters of the sea into a heap;
> He puts the depths into storehouses.
> Let the whole earth tremble before the LORD;
> let all the inhabitants of the world stand in awe of Him.
> For He spoke, and it came into being;
> He commanded, and it came into existence.
>
> PSALM 33:6-9

Brenda: *I am 53 and find that I am thrust into leadership roles with younger women a lot. My one question would be: Beth, what are the 10 most important things you would want to impart to someone you were mentoring?*

Beth: *To conserve space, how about five that can become springboards for a life well-lived and calling fulfilled? Pray continually and fervently ...*
1) For Jesus to be the love of your life and driving desire of your heart.
2) For a supernatural desire to study Scripture and for Jesus to open your mind to understand it (Luke 24:45).
3) For a supernatural love for others.
4) For knowledge of His will (Col.1:9-11).
5) For a deep grasp of grace. This helps us to be humble and forgiving.

ALLOW THE DIVINE PAIRING OF WORD AND BREATH TO STAY AWHIRL IN YOUR THOUGHTS WHILE YOU READ AND WRITE 2 TIMOTHY 3:14-17 IN THE BACK OF YOUR BOOK.

What do the first six words of 2 Timothy 3:16 tell you?

The Bible is God created

The Greek translated "inspired by God" in the HCSB and NASB is *theopneustos*.

The adjective *theopneustos* (only here in the New Testament) is compounded of *theos*, "God," and the verb *pneō*, "breathe."

You can see a more literal translation of it in the NIV: "All Scripture is God-breathed." Let's do some cross-referencing. The closest parallel in the New Testament was penned by the apostle Peter in 2 Peter 1:19-21.

Read the segment and record how the prophetic word landed on the page.

READ HEBREWS 4:12 AND FILL IN THE BLANKS. The word of God is ___*alive*___ and ___*active*___.

Write John 6:63 in this space.

The Spirit gives life; the flesh counts for nothing. The words I have spoken to you- they are full of the spirit + life.

From the opening of Genesis to the closing of Revelation, the words of God are upheld as utterly authoritative, appraised not simply as true but as *the* unwavering, immutable, unstoppable *Truth*. Not one word is empty. Not one word tumbles haphazardly to the ground. Every prophecy in Scripture is treated by Scripture with absolute, resolute expectancy. As God emphatically stated to the prophet Jeremiah, "I watch over My word to accomplish it" (Jer. 1:12).

Second Timothy 3:16 claims succinctly and exquisitely what is conveyed throughout the entire canon. This single verse communicates what sets the Bible apart from any other book held dear and sacred by other world religions. When you open your Bible, the words inside are not just bone-dry ink on thin-grade paper. They are living words, warm with the breath of God. This book is no museum of ancient documents. Many downcast believers who want so much to love the Bible and find it exciting confess with considerable self-condemnation, they simply do not.

("It) just doesn't do anything for me."

Countless problems seem to have no earthly solutions but we can praise God this is not one of them. Circle the word "it" in the indented quote and celebrate the best news a bored Bible student can get. "It" has no life and power of its own. God does. The reason "it" can affect us, transform us, renew us, and stir up our faith is because God who authored it activates it. The life of the Word is the Holy Spirit. Without Him, an animated word becomes an automated word. God didn't forsake the page and move on to His next best seller when the canon of Scripture was complete. God's Word is eternal (Ps. 119:89). He's still right there.

> The life of the Word is the Holy Spirit.

When Paul compounded the word *God-breathed*, he used a word of titanic importance in the Bible.

Read Genesis 1:1-2 and record what was hovering over the waters:

The breath of God.
Spirit

Ruah Elohim, Spirit of God. The Hebrew word *ruah* means *breath, wind, spirit.* Spirit and breath are not synonymous or reversible in meaning, so every time Scripture talks about wind or breath, it is not always in reference to the Spirit of God. However, the Spirit of God often works similarly. This was certainly true in regard to the inspiration of Scripture as told to us in 2 Timothy 3:16. I love the word picture of the canonical prophets being moved or carried along by the Holy Spirit in 2 Peter 1:21. Imagine the breath of God moving on those men driving their quills across a scroll.

When we deliberately engage with the Author, the same breath of God can blow the dust off our Bibles, bring those words to life, and put those words to work. What Paul wrote to the Thessalonians centuries ago is equally true for us.

> And we also thank God constantly for this, that when you
> received the word of God, which you heard from us, you
> accepted it not as the word of men but as what it really is,
> the word of God, which is at work in you believers.
> **1 THESSALONIANS 2:13, ESV**

How we accept the Word of God profoundly affects how we receive the work of God. Approaching Scripture with esteem, accepting its divine origin and authority, and expecting God to reveal Himself through it attaches faith to our encounter. It doesn't turn the Word into a vending machine. We may be certain of this: God shamelessly prizes faith.

REREAD 2 TIMOTHY 3:16-17 AND FILL IN THE REMAINDER OF THIS VISUAL BEGINNING WITH A DRAWING REPRESENTING THE BREATH OF GOD AND ENDING WITH THE TWO FINAL WORDS OF VERSE 17.

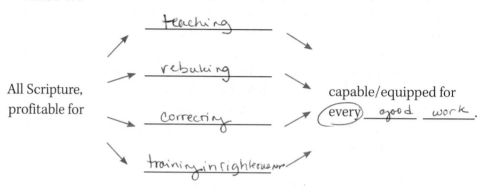

All Scripture, profitable for

teaching

rebuking

Correcting

training in righteousness

capable/equipped for every good work.

Circle the word *every*. That means we are equipped and made capable by Scripture even for good works that don't necessitate sharing the Word. Scripture is just as strategic for equipping the man or woman of God who works in government, stays home with the kids, or fixes car engines. That's the power of it. The Word of God works wherever the person of God works.

We'll spend the remainder of our time today finishing the diagram we began in our previous lesson with 2 Timothy 3:14-15 as our guide. Reread the verses. Timothy had been acquainted with the Scriptures since ___infancy___.

The Word of God works wherever the person of God works.

Perhaps your experience is similar to Timothy's or maybe you've only recently become acquainted. Either way testifies to God's gracious pursuit of you, my friend. Our depth of affection is not dependent on our length of acquaintance. Celebrate whatever point God began to woo you into the study of His Word and mark it on the diagram (page 135) by drawing this symbol:

Paul's reference in 2 Timothy 3:14 to those who'd acquainted Timothy with Scripture would have included but perhaps was not limited to Lois and Eunice.

Who has God used to acquaint you with Scripture and equip you for your calling? The five arrows on the top of the diagram are for the individuals who have been most formational in your spiritual life. Fill in up to five names. If you've only recently become acquainted with the Bible, don't fret if you only have less than five names. Over time, I'm sure you'll add others. (Remember, it is crucial to study under numerous teachers for checks and balances and so we don't derail if our main influencer does.)

If you'd like to go a step further and increase your appreciation of how God has used each of them, jot a specific emphasis or impartation from that teacher on the line of the arrow. For example, three of mine are Mary King, Marge Caldwell, and Buddy Walters. Mrs. King especially imparted love for missions through the Scriptures; Marge, love for Jesus Himself; and Buddy, spiritual disciplines and love for in-depth study.

Let's do one more thing and we'll call it a day. The space beneath the diagram is provided for documenting elements that were part of your natural upbringing and development rather than spiritual. In and of themselves, they may seem to have little connection to God and to your calling but my hope is that you will see how He wastes nothing. Timothy's mixed heritage was leveraged for the gospel. Your parents and primary influencers don't have to be Christians to impart skills and experiences God integrates into your calling. Those have a place in your panoramic picture. You may have lived abroad or in the inner city or had a sibling with Down syndrome. You may have possessed a natural talent. Placed in the hands of the Potter, elements like these become added colors and textures of clay He uses to shape us into unique vessels.

Perhaps your parents divorced or, like my husband, your family endured a tragedy. Not one whit of the experience need be good for a merciful God to use it for good. He can rob the darkness of the gain of your pain and redeem it powerfully in the light.

Conclude now with documentation on the diagram of particularly formative experiences that grew out of the natural soil of your life. Fill the space to illustrate what has made you *you*.

Group Session Five

WATCH THE VIDEO—FULFILL YOUR MINISTRY

INTRODUCTION

Today's session will suspend us right between the third and fourth chapters of 2 Timothy, offering us a panoramic view of the complexity and camaraderie of a servant's life on a crowded planet.

"Servants" in 1 Corinthians 4:1: Greek *hupērétēs;* masculine noun from *hupó*, __under__, beneath and *erétēs*, a __rower__.

A subordinate, servant, attendant, or assistant in general. The subordinate official who waits to accomplish the commands of his superior.

In classical Greek, a __Common__ __sailor__, as distinguished from, a seaman, sailor.

1. __Rowers__ don't __build__ __up__ and maintain muscle by __rowing__ __downstream__.

Easy for you to say

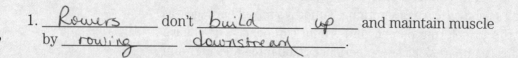

Epi sterizo Steroid

2. Staying in __rythm__ and __sync__ with a __team__ takes __concentrated__ __effort__.

Mark 15:21

3. _Rowing_ also necessitates a certain _amount_ of _repitition_ .

4. _Rower's_ have each _others_ _backs_ .

Fulfill Your Ministry

Day One

BEYOND INCONVENIENCE

FLASH FORWARD: *Proclaim the message; persist in it whether convenient or not; rebuke, correct, and encourage with great patience and teaching.*
2 TIMOTHY 4:2

Today we begin the end of our journey as Paul begins the end of the letter. The close has come too swiftly, the letter too brief for some of our tastes. Paul had written far longer letters. His letter to the Romans and his first letter to the Corinthians both contained more than 6,500 words. We wish he'd tarried here like he'd tarried there. But in this final letter, only 1,200 or so words spilled from the quill of a man running out of time. The document had a thousand miles to travel to reach the palm of its recipient, and its recipient a thousand miles to travel if Paul was to see his face one last time.

As 2 Timothy 4 opens, Paul knows he's narrowing the letter to a close. You can see it in his words. Listen and you'll hear it in his tone.

PLEASE READ VERSES 1-2 AND HANDWRITE THEM IN THE BACK OF YOUR BOOK.

Behold the changing of the guard. The letter was not the only thing the apostle intended to place in Timothy's hands. He placed his ministry of the gospel, dearer to him than his own skin, in the young man's hands. The Greek *diamartyromai* translated

> *"to solemnly charge," can be a technical term for taking an oath … it can also be a technical term for the transfer of office, which is what is happening as Paul knows his life is ending and Timothy will have to shoulder the responsibility without him. It can be a technical term for judgment in a law court as well (BAGD 452 [4b]).*[1]

Paul issued earlier charges to Timothy (1 Tim. 5:21; 6:13), and did so in a similar oath-like style, boldly naming God and Christ as witnesses. The charge we read in 2 Timothy 4:1, however, carries the full weight of a last will and testament.

Paul loved Timothy. He trusted him. But the young pastor hadn't been knocked to the ground and blinded by a lightning bolt from heaven. He hadn't heard the Lord's voice crack through the atmosphere and call out his name. Paul had. Timothy needed to know what we also yearn to know: the call of Christ can come differently but Christ who calls is exactly the same. Paul's charge to Timothy was not delivered in obscurity. It was not whispered between the two of them in secret or confined to the eyes of a letter's sender and receiver. The official transaction was held in public view of heaven in the very presence of God and Christ. Paul issued the oath in the bright light of three future realities:

1. Christ's judgment of the living and the dead,

2. Christ's appearing,

3. Christ's kingdom.

What happens now matters then, Timothy. Every present moment has future implications. This is not about your past. Not just about your present. This is about your future. Everyone's future. This will all matter. This will be what you will wish you had done. So do it. Because what happens now matters then.

> Every present moment has future implications.

At the end of the age, Jesus will judge believers and unbelievers alike but with divergent objectives.

First Corinthians 3:10-15 and 2 Corinthians 5:6-10 explain the purpose of believers' judgment. Summarize it here:

> we share salvation as believers. but we will be judged by what we do in Jesus name - are we faithful? Blessing others? Sharing the Gospel?

Revelation 20:11-15 records the judgment of unbelievers. Please read the segment and record what will take place.

> all will be judged - If you were not in kingdom family in life you will not be in death.

Disturbing, isn't it? In one of the most stunning scenes in Scripture, God shares with his servant Abraham His plans to inspect Sodom and Gomorrah because the outcry over their grievous sins was great (Gen. 18:16-33) Abraham, in instant angst over his nephew's family in Sodom, launches into a daring inquisition: *Will You really sweep away the righteous with the wicked? Won't the Judge of all the earth do what is just? Would You spare the city for 50 righteous?*

Yes, God replies. *For 45?* Yes. *40? 30? 20? 10?* Yes. In the end, Sodom proved utterly saturated by evil, and as Lot, his wife, and daughters lingered, God seized them so they could escape the city's destruction. Will the Judge of all the earth do what is just? The answer is yes. All who trust in Jesus are justified by His blood and saved from the wrath to come (Rom. 5:9).

The judgment of unbelievers at the great white throne will settle their eternal destiny. The judgment of believers will concern their reward or loss of reward based on God's evaluation of their works. Fire is an agent in both judgments but for very different purposes. The fire at the judgment seat for believers will be for the sake of revelation, putting every work to the test, not for quantity but for quality, showing what lasts. Wood, hay, and straw represent temporal works that will quickly burn away. Gold, silver, and precious stones represent eternal works that will outlast the flames.

Our present works don't only affect future rewards. They affect future assignments. As surely as Christ appeared in flesh and blood, He will again appear, crowned in glory and robed in majesty to usher in His kingdom. We will not be ghosts wafting around a ghost town. We will be have fully alive bodies on a fully alive earth where we will thrive at fully alive posts. In Matthew 25:14, Jesus taught that the kingdom of heaven will be "like a man going on a journey, who called his servants and entrusted to them his property" (ESV). The name of this study, the primary concept that has driven us for weeks, is tucked into that verse. Circle it please.

In the parable He used as a kingdom parallel, each servant's responsibility was to steward the master's property well. "Now after a long time," the master returned and settled accounts (Matt. 25:19, ESV). Each servant who'd faithfully invested the small amount of property entrusted to him was commended then placed over much, sharing the master's happiness. The servants weren't expected to be trustworthy with what they hadn't been given. They weren't judged by comparison or graded on the curve. The only question on the master's table was this: what did you do with what I entrusted to you?

What happens now matters then.

Because what happens now matters then.

Note the high-pitched string of imperatives in 2 Timothy 4:2. Reduce as many of them as you can to one-word exclamations. I'll get you started.

Preach!

Be prepared to shaw all the time — to be prepared we need to keep studying too

Correct

rebuke

Encourage

Be patient

Second Timothy 4:2 takes the enormous tension of ministry and stuffs it into a nutshell: be urgent ... and patient. Urgent with the gospel. Patient with the people.

> **When did you last feel the tension between urgency for someone to embrace the ways of Jesus and patience with them in their upheaval until they did?**
>
> *Rowon — 1 week ago*

> **What was the most challenging part of maintaining the tension?**
>
> *I wanted her to pray & be open for Holy Spirit she said she was not ready*

Two Greek words express the general idea of patience but the distinction between them is sublime. *"Makrothumía is patience in respect to persons while hupomonē, endurance, is putting up with things or circumstances."*[2]

> **Which do you find more challenging: bearing up with people or circumstances? Why?**
>
> *Both! Ipeople because I want to "see" them Circumstances because I lack faith*

But the fruit of the
Spirit is love, joy,
peace, (patience),
kindness, goodness,
faith, gentleness, self-
control. Against such
things there is no law.

GALATIANS 5:22-23

I'm fairly confident about responding *me, too*. If you find circumstances harder to endure than people, however, either your circumstances are harder than mine or my people are harder than yours. We could each use prayer! In ancient Greek terms, being patient with people requires its own brand of endurance. After all, people are easier to blame and harder to forgive. It's not surprising then, that, of the two Greek words, the one included in the fruit of the Spirit is *makrothumia*, patience regarding people. Circle the word in Galatians 5:22-23 in the margin.

> **Check the page of your Bible and record how many verses separate 2 Timothy 3:16 and 2 Timothy 4:2.**
>
> *2*

The similarities between them are no doubt intentional. If Timothy would faithfully preach the word, he'd also faithfully rebuke, correct, encourage, and teach because the Word empowered by the Spirit would do its job. Rebuking and correcting in the name of God without the Spirit of God makes people recoil from God.

We are not all called to preach sermons or teach a Bible study class, but remember, we are all called to study Scriptures and to communicate the gospel. Therefore, these verses can also apply to us. I learned something fascinating that I think will intrigue you, too. The four uses of Scripture named in 2 Timothy 3:16 (and closely echoed in 2 Timothy 4:2) "include both priestly and prophetic roles ... patterned on rabbinic uses of Torah."[3] According to this rabbinical approach, teaching and training were considered to be priestly functions. Rebuking and correcting were more often prophetic functions. Priests sympathized with human weakness. Prophets warned when weakness could also be their downfall. We need both.

Name a time when you desperately needed the ministry of God's Word in a priestly fashion.

Frieda Cowling – when I came to Christ or back to Christ in March 2015

Name a time when you needed the word in a prophetic fashion.

Paula Prussel – when I was cheating on my first husband!

Sometimes we need both approaches just to get through one day.

READ 2 TIMOTHY 4:2 ONCE MORE IN THE MARGIN. Draw a rectangle around the phrase "convenient or not." The Greek reads *eukairōs akairōs*. Here's how it's worded in two other translations:

In season and out of season (ESV).

Whether the time is favorable or not (NLT).

PERSIST. As we share our last few lessons, I so want to give you whatever I have. I lack so much. I'm still on such a learning curve. But this much I know after three decades of ministry: pure persistence will carry you where no amount of talent, skill, aptitude, and experience can. Persistence will take you where all the networking and name-dropping in Christendom cannot go

Proclaim the message; persist in it whether convenient or not; rebuke, correct, and encourage with great patience and teaching.

2 TIMOTHY 4:2

because persistence still has you on your feet when the majority hit the couch over the next inconvenience. Persist …

When it seems the anointing has run completely dry.

When it seems heaven has forgotten you're alive.

When you feel uninspired. Tired. When you've been fired.

When your faith shows no results.

When your obedience has not paid off.

When your prayers seem like wasted breath.

When your bones feel dead—and so does the Word.

You have not wasted a single breath on prayer.

Persist. Jesus is on His way. Your anointing has not run dry. Heaven has not forgotten you're alive. You have not believed for nothing. The results of your faith will soon sprout from that fallow ground. Just a little more rain. Just a little more thunder. Your obedience will pay off. You have not wasted a single breath on prayer. There is still life in your bones and, child of God, there is still life in His Word. Persist.

Things on My Mind, Part 1

Personal reflections at the end of a class are some of my favorite moments. After absorbing the material over a good amount of time, finally you have a bird's-eye view of the content and can speak to the themes you think are most prominent and most relevant. In that spirit, I'd like to wrap up these months with Timothy with a pretty simple conversation. These are the things on my mind.

I. BE GENTLE TO EVERYONE, ABLE TO TEACH (2 TIM. 2:24).

I'm struck by this letter's call to bold teaching and preaching, and the careful transmission of the gospel alongside its simultaneous emphasis on a kind, non-quarrelsome, patient, and gentle manner (2:24-5). Paul instructs Timothy to "reject foolish and ignorant disputes, knowing that they breed quarrels" (2:23). I'm typing these words during an election season when basically every single conversation is foolish and disputatious. I refuse to accept that this means avoiding or ending conversations altogether. For me it must mean boldly seeking more fruitful and charitable conversations, especially about things that matter.

If we are truly going to preach the gospel in our generation, we must learn how to have better, saner conversations with people. The first step toward this goal is to learn to listen.

In *Becoming Wise*, Krista Tippett suggests that our culture in general has neglected the art of listening and must learn it anew.[1] Using the language of Rachel Naomi Remen, Tippett explains "generous listening" like this:

"Listening is more than being quiet while the other person speaks until you can say what you have to say ... Generous listening is powered by curiosity, a virtue we can invite and nurture in ourselves to render it instinctive. It involves a kind of vulnerability—a willingness to be surprised, to let go of assumptions and take in ambiguity. The listener wants to understand the humanity behind the words of the other, and patiently summons one's own best self and one's own best words and questions."[2]

When we are not ashamed of the gospel, we have the freedom to ask good questions and listen to other people well. We are faithful to the tradition we've received but the bottom line is not protecting our big egos. We keep reading Scripture carefully, proving ourselves to be ones who carefully handle the word of truth (2:15), and we are not threatened by any worldview or perspective. We do not have to let go of our Christian convictions to actually hear somebody out. We are unashamed in our message; we proclaim it, persist in it, whether it is convenient or not (2 Tim. 4:2), and we do this with kindness and patience. Generous listening is a revolutionary act of kindness in a world of screaming and competing voices.

II. LOVERS OF SELF (2 TIM. 3:1)

One of the lines in this epistle that will stick with me is: "But mark this: There will be terrible times in the last days. People will be lovers of themselves ... without love" (2 Tim. 3:1-3, NIV). Timothy was called to preach the word with patience and careful instruction during a time when folks were swayed by wrong desires (3:6) even gathering teachers "to suit their own desires" (4:3, NIV). Paul exhorted Timothy to "flee the evil desires of youth" and "pursue righteousness, faith, love and peace" (2:22, NIV), to keep his head in all situations (4:5).

In David Kinnaman and Gabe Lyons' book *Good Faith: Being a Christian When Society Thinks You're Irrelevant*, they present results from a 2015 Barna study. The study shows, among other things, that 72 percent of practicing Christians agreed (either completely or somewhat) with the following statement: "To be fulfilled in life, you should pursue the things you desire most." The study also showed that 66 percent of practicing Christians agreed (either completely or somewhat) with this: "The highest goal of life is to enjoy it as much as possible." It's good to have the data, but I doubt we needed to see it to believe Christians' priorities were askew. What is extraordinary is that the church doesn't seem to be bothered by the embarrassing disparity of claiming to follow Jesus while holding the dead idols of self in our hands. Kinnaman and Lyons suggest:

> "The morality of self-fulfillment is everywhere, like the air we breathe. Much of the time we don't even notice we're constantly bombarded with messages that reinforce self-fulfillment ... Me focused morality is all the rage ... the morality of self-fulfillment has even crept into American Christianity. Large percentages of practicing Christians embrace the principles of the new moral code."[3]

Paul's call to Timothy, in stark contrast, was to give himself away completely and thereby gain everything that matters. The highest goal in life, according to 2 Timothy, is not to merely enjoy ourselves, but to fulfill our calling by faithfully proclaiming the gospel to the glory of God.

> *"You, however, be self-controlled in all things, endure hardship, do an evangelist's work, fulfill your ministry" (2 Tim. 4:5, NET).*

"Timothy is called to total commitment ... His tough assignment demands self-denial, self-discipline, and self-commitment."[4] I do not believe that pleasure is evil or that our desires are evil. I do believe our desires need an informed and discerning sorting and sifting. The better I know myself the more reluctant I am to pray unreservedly for God to give me the desires of my heart.

Most of my praying these days is that God will transform my desires so that I can live a life that is pleasing to Him, thus also fulfilling me.

I trust the desires in my heart that are pleasing to Him will remain, that He will refine the ones that are not, and that He will ultimately fulfill the ones that last. Now, I well know there's a significant tension here, so much so that even the psalmist can say, "Take delight in the LORD, and he will give you the desires of your heart" (Ps. 37:4, NIV). Still, I don't mind overstating the case, because I don't think too many of us in the American church are in danger of neglecting our desires or pursuing too little pleasure. I'm certainly not. However you choose to articulate this tension, I think we can all agree that the life to which Paul calls Timothy, and so also us, is one that will involve some denial of self.

Day Two

AN ITCH TO HEAR

FLASH FORWARD: *For the time will come when they will not tolerate sound doctrine, but according to their own desires, will multiply teachers for themselves because they have an itch to hear something new.* **2 TIMOTHY 4:3**

Our ridiculously loved birddog, Geli (short for Angelina), recently lost her right eye to a raccoon. Keith was out of town, so the day Geli wouldn't stop pawing her face, I was tasked with holding her head still and forcing the lid open. I expected to see a fleck of dirt. Instead I saw an eyeball that no longer possessed an iris or a pupil. It looked like a bluish-white marble bearing three indentions. Within hours the lid would no longer close—I'm still traumatized at the thought of it. I should speak a word in memoriam for the raccoon I soon discovered in our yard. Geli had obviously cornered it and the critter went straight for her eye in self-defense. In reciprocal self-defense, with a side order of vengeance, Geli sent it to its final rest. Country living is not for the faint of heart. I sobbed so hard at the veterinary clinic, it's a wonder no one in the waiting room posted a video online.

Queen Esther, "Star" for short, has never been the same. She's my border collie and constant shadow. Keith and I got both puppies eight years ago and raised them together and, while they're both quirky, the Queen's codependency issues win by a landslide. After the raccoon incident, she proceeded to make her life's aim becoming Geli's right eye. From the moment Geli was released to romp again through our woods, Star ran to the right side of her, skin-to-skin, herding her around trees, broken limbs, and holes like they were competing in an obstacle course for pairs. Geli appreciated it and submitted to it for a few weeks, until Star got so bossy and irritable, the birddog couldn't take it anymore. She then did what she'd been capable of doing all eight years. She picked up speed with her long, lithe legs and left the short-legged Queen in the dust. Star plopped down by my side, sulking. I squeezed her around the neck and said, "You can't make her stay, Sweetie." I've thought about it a good bit since.

OUR NEXT SEGMENT IS 2 TIMOTHY 4:3-5. Please read and handwrite it on the appropriate page.

What phenomenon did Paul predict in verses 3-4?

False teachers - People will find someone who tells them what they want to hear.

These verses have been applied to spiritual climates of countless generations since the canon of Scripture was closed. Timothy had already caught glimpses of it in Ephesus as some who'd formerly walked in truth bafflingly turned aside to myths. John Calvin, the 16th century French theologian, spoke of it in his generation, "Many have itching ears; and in our natural vanity most men are more delighted by foolish allegories than by solid erudition."[4]

The "down-grade" controversy in the 1880s between Charles Haddon Spurgeon and the Baptist Union occurred over his concerns that doctrine was slipping by popular demand. So, what else is new? Wait a minute. Does something about this discussion ring a bell? Let's pull back out a concept we discussed in Week Four by reading Matthew 24:3-8.

According to verse 8, what did Jesus say the fulfillment of the prophecies in verses 4-7 would mean?

The beginning of the end

The parallel is marked by two implicit characteristics: increasing frequency and intensity. This means what we're observing today could pale in comparison to the world Jesus-followers a century from now will be challenged to serve.

Nevertheless, do you think we have verifiable grounds to claim that the demand for novelty and for teaching to scratch itching ears has intensified in the last 20 years? If so, offer two examples as support.

Yes - Joel Olsteen for example - ALQueda - Jim Jones - I think the digital age has exponentially encouraged this

Generations throughout New Testament history have had justifiable claims on the climate of 2 Timothy 4:4-5, but what spikes the needle on the graph in ours is unlimited access to teachers. We have teachers by the thousands and teachings by the tens of thousands right at our fingertips, audio or video, full-screen or split-screen. Praise God we do. Access to authentic discipleship is exploding in this era of history, I believe, to arm the people of God with the sword of the Spirit so we can stand valiantly in truth and pierce the darkness. Of course, with unlimited access to truth comes unlimited access to skewed theologies. To strange teachings. To misapplied doctrines. And to absolute myths.

One element many of us enjoy most in our access to innumerable podcasts is the ability to order one up like we order a specialty drink at Starbucks®. We can tailor it to our tastes by choosing the topic, the kind of teacher we want, and the length we will listen to. And, if in three minutes we don't like how it tastes, we're one click away from another.

I won't kid you. I love options. But customized theology is dangerous. I'm not knocking topic shopping. I've done it numerous times and often received a needed word. But if all we do is topic shop, let's face it, most of us probably aren't going to search the category "Solid Erudition."

Word Biblical Commentary offers a translation of the Greek in 2 Timothy 4:3a with a key adjective: "For a time will come when they will not put up with healthy teaching."[5]

We sometimes limit our discipleship to topic shopping in order to tailor the teaching to our desire. The problem is that what we want is not always what we need. The trouble with always going for something new is the likelihood we're trying to outrun something old. That's the trendy version of "always learning and never able to come to a knowledge of the truth" (2 Tim. 3:7). The irony of making relevance the goal is that it inadvertently leads to irrelevance.

The Great Physician inscribed a prescription for optimum health:

> All Scripture is inspired by God and is profitable for teaching,
> for rebuking, for correcting, for training in righteousness.
> **2 TIMOTHY 3:16**

God originated customization. He knows exactly what word He needs to send forth to heal us (Ps. 107:20). If all we receive is teaching and training, our spiritual health will suffer. The same is true if all we receive is rebuke and correction. To drive it home, let's make the same point again by using 2 Timothy 4:2:

> Proclaim the message … rebuke, correct, and
> encourage with great patience and teaching.

If we're only rebuked and corrected and never encouraged with great patience and teaching, our spiritual health will not thrive. The reverse is equally accurate. Write it here.

If we are ~~always~~ only encouraged + taught our spiritual walk will suffer

> The irony of making relevance the goal is that it inadvertently leads to irrelevance.

Christy: *How do you consistently put God first and obey Him, instead of giving in to busyness, laziness, the desire for comfort and safety, wanting to keep everyone happy, fear, etc.?*

Beth: *I have to stay on guard against those tendencies, too, but what helps me stay closely engaged with Jesus is having lived long enough to learn what happens when I don't. I need Him too badly and have made too much of a mess of my life in the past to not prioritize Him. I'm also just simply not happy when I've put something or someone else first. I slip into performance and approval traps, my joy drains and my anxiety level rises until it nearly drowns me. I get gossipy, critical, and miserably insecure. Truly, Jesus is all that makes my life work. It goes completely awry when He's not driving it.*

We've stumbled onto a reason why sitting regularly under preaching and teaching in a sound local church is crucial. We often have no idea what messages our pastors and teachers will bring. All we know is that we're heading to church and, whatever the Lord offers, we want to receive. Maybe we get out of our cars with hopes of being greatly encouraged but what we receive is a rebuke. And, lo and behold, it doesn't kill us; instead, repentance brings us back to life. Sometimes we feel defeated and brace ourselves for the rebuke we think we deserve. But the word from the pulpit is drenched in encouragement, splashing us in the grace we need to get back up.

We are immeasurably blessed to live in a discipleship era in which we can choose books, podcasts, and conferences thematically to grow in specific areas of need and responsibility. However, we must also hang on for dear life to pastors and teachers who will "not shrink back from declaring to [us] the whole counsel of God" (Acts 20:27, ESV).

If you're a fellow Bible teacher, how does this concept of "healthy teaching" apply from our side of the podium?

Let's study hard. Let's pursue accurate teaching at all costs. And, like Star with Geli, we'll do considerably less sulking if, in the ebb and flow of class size, we keep in mind we cannot make them stay.

Itching ears have gone viral but we'll fall into false assumptions if we conclude that any lesson that makes us feel good is automatically bad doctrine or that every lesson that makes us feel bad must be good. If the gospel isn't good news, it needs a new name.

GAZE AT THE BREATHTAKING SCENE IN NEHEMIAH 8:9-12.
Summarize the (appropriate!) initial response of the Israelites and their transition under the instruction of their faithful leaders.

Laws bring a yoke - a weight - at first seem oppressive - as "laws" are explained we usually see they are for our good -

Sound teaching of Scripture cuts to the heart and also mends it. Sometimes it is hard to swallow and other times it slides down the throat like honey from the comb. Sometimes the same word that makes us cry turns our weeping into dancing. Isn't this one of the things that makes us love the Bible so? One among countless things that make it like no other book on earth?

Write Jeremiah 15:16 in this space.

When your words came I ate them; they were my joy and my hearts delight, find bear your name Lord God almighty

Read 2 Timothy 4:5 again as we close. Though people will increasingly want their itching ears scratched instead of healed (Matt. 13:15), Paul exhorted Timothy, "But you, keep your head in all situations" (2 Tim. 4:5, NIV).

Does *keep your head* have any particular application to you presently? If so, share. *I am pulled in lots of directions very busy I need to ① keep God first in all situations ② remember I am a kingdom citizen*

The HCSB, NASB, and ESV wrap up the exhortation with three powerful words: "fulfill your ministry." In case a fresh reminder that all who follow Jesus are called to ministry is due, read Ephesians 4:11-12 in the ESV:

> And [Jesus] gave the apostles, the prophets, the evangelists,
> the shepherds and teachers, to equip the saints for the
> work of ministry, for building up the body of Christ.

We are saints called to the work of ministry, equipped by the Word and by Christ-gifted leaders. Our ministries—in all their God-intended diversities and seasons—are supreme reasons we're here on this planet. Not one of us is gift-less or purposeless. Not one of us is missing a ministry.

You, _____Ramona_____, fulfill yours. Exhort me to fulfill mine. No one can do it for us. Let's forsake trying to do someone else's ministry and just fulfill our own. In so doing, we will certainly endure hardship and, whether or not we have the gifting of an evangelist, often do the work of an evangelist, sharing Christ's glorious gospel. Oh, that God will use these five weeks to burn in our hearts the unquenchable passion and holy determination of Paul.

> I do not account my life of any value nor as precious
> to myself, if only I may finish my course and the
> ministry that I received from the Lord Jesus.
> ACTS 20:24, ESV

Our lives are of unspeakable value to God. We are precious to Him. Let's settle that matter so an overdeveloped preciousness to self does not end up protecting us from our own divine purpose. We don't have long here. We don't have time to waste on infighting, foolishness, and fear. We don't have months to drum up the approval of all our peers. We don't have years to keep procrastinating. Let's not just plan to do what it takes. Let's do what it takes. The joy of the Lord, my friend, is our strength.

Not one of us is gift-less or purposeless.

Day Three

EVERY LAST DROP

FLASH FORWARD: *For I am already being poured out as a drink offering, and the time for my departure is close.* **2 TIMOTHY 4:6**

My memory of the last time I sat next to my mentor in church is as vivid as yesterday. Marge and I often sat together in meetings but we normally landed on opposite sides of our large sanctuary on Sunday mornings. Keith and I raised our daughters from toddlerhood in that church so we formed the habit of sitting in the section closest to the children's departments. This particular Sunday about 11 years ago, Keith was away and I planted myself beside this extraordinary woman who'd profoundly influenced my ministry life for two decades.

We held hands for a while that day in the service, this middle-aged woman and her 90-year-old mentor. I'd placed my hand on hers and she'd turned her palm upward and clasped it. Moments like those aren't wasted on me. I stared at our hands, awake to the grace of having been loved by her so long.

We observed the Lord's Supper an hour later. My head was bowed but my eyes were open as a deacon voiced the blessing over the cup. I glanced to the side and saw the tiny communion glass in Marge's unsteady hand tip over and spill in her lap, sparing only a drop. I wanted so badly to prop the cup back up before she opened her eyes but the brevity of the prayer prevented it. I looked away, hoping to minimize any awkwardness. She recovered quickly and consumed what was left but I did not recover for days. Whether the sight of that spilled cup had any God-intended significance, I do not know. I only know that the inevitability of her well-run race nearing its end was inescapable and overwhelming for this spiritual daughter.

PLEASE READ 2 TIMOTHY 4:6-8 AND WRITE IT IN THE BACK OF YOUR WORKBOOK. Compare 2 Timothy 4:6, written in Paul's final imprisonment in Rome, to Philippians 2:17 written in his first. What metaphor do they have in common?

Poured out like an offering

How do the uses differ?

to show faith vs end of life

Even in Paul's final days, with body and heart scarred by rejection and persecution from his own people, his Jewish heritage was precious to him. He had taken the gospel to the Gentiles but he had not taken the Jews from the gospel. He wasn't meant to. Judaism was the crib of the gospel. Paul's Jewish Messiah had come, not to condemn the law but to fulfill it. Threads of ceremonial language are stitched with distinct color into the fabric of the apostle's letters. Paul's imagery in 2 Timothy 4:6 loops all the way back to the sacrificial system instituted by God in Exodus.

READ GOD'S INSTRUCTIONS FOR PRIESTS IN EXODUS 29:38-43.
What liquid comprised the drink offering? Record additional points of significance in the margin.

wine

READ NUMBERS 28:16-24. What occasion did the instructions involve?

Passover

In verse 24, with what was the drink offering coupled?

The regular offerings

How do the following verses written by Paul bring profound meaning to the sacrifices prescribed in the previous segments?
EPHESIANS 5:1-2

Jesus was the Lamb - goat - sacrificial animal

1 CORINTHIANS 5:7

Keeping those in mind, reflect on 2 Timothy 4:6 again in light of the commentary excerpt in the margin.

Totally expended. Poured out. So worthy was Jesus, the Passover Lamb, that Paul pictured his life as a voluntary drink offering spilling out on the altar of sacrifice. He would not stop until every drop fell and the vessel was dry.

Paul was aware that he was slowly dying. Imagine being chained not only to the floor but to the daily dread of martyrdom. Perhaps he knew he'd die by the sword. If not, an entire range of options could have harassed his thoughts.

do this morning or the start of your day + evening — Bookend your day + in time w/ God. pass this down to your children —

[Paul] compared the pouring out of his energy in ministry to the pouring out of the wine of an Old Testament drink offering. Such offerings ... were totally expended or poured out as an accompaniment to the burnt offering in the sanctuary (Num 28:7). Paul had used this metaphor in Phil 2:17. The present tense of the verb for "being poured out" suggests Paul's awareness that this was an act then underway. Paul was aware that he was slowly dying in God's service, and he felt that the shedding of his blood in martyrdom would complete the drink offering to God. He viewed the entire ordeal as a libation to God.[6]

After all, the Roman government of his era "thought it necessary to rule by terror."[7] Emperor Nero was notorious for making a sport of torture. According to the historian Tacitus who was alive in Rome at the time of Christian persecution,

And in their deaths they were made the subjects of sport: for they were covered with the hides of wild beasts, and worried to death by dogs, or nailed to crosses, or set fire to, and when the day declined, burnt to serve for nocturnal lights. Nero offered his own gardens for the spectacle. [8]

GLANCE AHEAD TO 2 TIMOTHY 4:9 AND COUPLE IT WITH 2 TIMOTHY 4:6. On what basis can you assume Paul was aware that his death was imminent yet might not be immediate?

Come quickly & I am ebbing away daily

For I am already being poured out as a drink offering, and the time for my ___departure___ is close. (2 Tim. 4:6) (Fill in the blank.)

The word for "departure" is analysis *(only here in the NT). It comes from the verb* analyō, *which literally meant "unloose." The noun was used for the "loosing" of a vessel from its moorings or of soldiers "breaking up" camp for departure. Paul was about ready to "strike tent" (leave his physical body) and forsake this earth for the presence of his Lord.*[9]

Paul would soon be loosed. Loosed from the hardships and horrors of this world. Loosed from rejection and betrayal. From disappointment and despair. From pain and anxiety, hunger and sleeplessness. From heart-wrenching farewells.

By now you know Paul well enough to add several of your own.
He would be loosed from ...

beatings   loneliness   fear
torture   cold

> When our God-appointed times come and our beating hearts still, death will not mean losing. It will mean loosing.

The tentmaker would strike his final tent. The sailor's vessel would be loosed from its moorings where it heaved and dove, battered by winds and waves. The soldier—a prisoner of a cosmic war—who'd led countless troops and pled against defection, would bend his aching body once more and break camp.

When our God-appointed times come and our beating hearts still, death will not mean losing. It will mean loosing. The gravity that pins our feet to this world has no hold on our souls. But until that day comes, we embrace our places here. Every common clay jar becomes as exquisite as an alabaster box when the life within pours out like a drink offering. Nothing poured out on the feet of Jesus is cheap perfume.

In 2 Timothy 4:7, Paul summarized thirty years in three moving phrases each expressed with perfect-tense verbs declaring finality. In Greek, "the objects are placed first to draw attention not to what Paul has done but to the fight, the race, and the faith that are the Lord's. This is emphasized by the use of the definite article 'the' before each object."[10]

Fill in the blanks to feel the force:

"the ___*departure is near*___ I have fought, the ___*good fight*___
I have completed, the ___*race*___ I have kept."[11]

Life is a fight (Greek: *agona*), but we can pick a good one. We can agonize over things we are not big enough to change or we can agonize for the sake of the One big enough to change us.

I have finished. Paul was able to know with crystal clarity that his goal in Acts 20:24—to finish his course and the ministry he'd received from Jesus—had been accomplished. Who can fathom what this meant to a man who, thirty years prior, sat sightless for three long days in a house on Straight Street in Damascus wondering what future would befall a persecutor?

I have kept the faith. This, above all other feats, is what God most esteems. We live by faith. We love by faith. If we gain everything and lose our faith, we've lost everything. If we lose everything but keep our faith, the sufferings of this present time will be unworthy of comparing to the glory we will receive (Rom. 8:18).

Bask in 2 Timothy 4:8 (NET):

> Finally the crown of righteousness is reserved for me. The
> Lord, the righteous Judge, will award it to me in that day.

"Paul says that a 'crown' awaits him. This is not *diadēma* ('diadem'), the royal crown, but *stephanos*, the laurel wreath given to the winner of the Marathon race (cf. 1 Cor 9:25)."[12]

What makes this wreath seem more fitting than a diadem?

a royal crown comes from station in life
a laurel wreath is hard won — hard hard won

Finally. Paul launched his ministry with the full expectancy of Christ's imminent return. No sooner had Paul received back his sight than he yearned to see the face of Christ. The Thessalonian letters written early in his tenure are chock-full of references to Christ's return. Paul longed for the One who had come to come again. This is the heart of having "loved His appearing" (v. 8). Though God's Word is eternal and each book planned and perfectly timed, the young Paul likely never imagined Jesus tarrying long enough for the old Paul to write something like the Pastoral Epistles.

NEARING OUR JOURNEY'S END, LET'S RETURN TO 1 TIMOTHY 3:14-15 AND RECAPTURE PAUL'S PURPOSE IN WRITING THE FIRST LETTER. What was it?

To teach how Christians are to behave

The church of the living God, the pillar and foundation of the truth would continue on. It would survive persecution, defection, rejection, oppression, infighting, reviling, and hiding. The church would survive misappropriation in medieval crusades and misuse in unholy wars. It would survive near-deification, reformation, and God only knows how much political exploitation. But the church *would* survive because it was Christ's. At times it might be quieted but it could not be killed.

The apostle chained to the floor in a Roman dungeon could be killed, however, and soon would be. This was his glorious consolation: *Finally ... the Lord.*

Day Four

A PAIR OF WAYFARERS

FLASH FORWARD: *Only Luke is with me. Bring Mark with you, for he is useful to me in the ministry.* **2 TIMOTHY 4:11**

I have kept the faith. At first blush, Paul's five autobiographical words in 2 Timothy 4:7 seem to say it all, especially in light of 1 John 5:4— "This is the victory that has conquered the world: our faith." Had Paul wrapped up his final letter just one verse later, speaking of the award he would receive from the righteous Judge, he would have gone out with a bang like fireworks on the 4th of July. However, because we have 2 Timothy 4:9-22, we know Paul's faith wasn't the only thing he kept. Paul kept his heart. To the very end, he lived his claim in 2 Corinthians 6:11 (ESV): "our heart is wide open." Wide open to love. Wide open to hurt. Wide open to loss. Every warm hello cracked open a door for a hard farewell.

PLEASE READ AND HANDWRITE 2 TIMOTHY 4:9-15 IN THE BACK OF YOUR BOOK.

Now broaden the scope to include verses 16-20 with this aim: to locate each city mentioned in 2 Timothy 4:9-20 on the map on the inside back cover and write near it the name the segment associates with it.

Since Demas, Crescens, Titus, and Tychicus departed from Rome toward their destinations, draw arrows from Rome to each of the cities you labeled with their names.

Whose departure was framed negatively?

Demas

The contrast with 2 Timothy 4:8 is almost certainly intentional. What two loves are mentioned just one verse apart?

Crown of righteousness vs. love of the world

How is Demas described in Philemon 24?

a fellow worker

FULFILL YOUR MINISTRY   165

Paul and Demas at one time had worked side-by-side for the gospel, but in the end, Demas heartbreakingly abandoned Paul and the faith. And we're only left to wonder if Demas ever returned.

Crescens and Titus most likely left Rome for ministry assignments. Scripture tells us nothing more about Crescens but we know much about Titus, whom Paul called a true son (Titus 1:4). Whether or not this father and son in the faith ever saw one another again or said their own farewells is unknown.

How does 2 Corinthians 7:5-6 make the absence of Titus in the closing chapter of Paul's life particularly poignant?

Titus comforted Paul - or God comforted Paul thru Titus.

Who did Paul tell Timothy to bring with him? What reason did he give for the summons?

Mark. Because he helped Paul in his ministry

That solitary sentence tells us a scroll-full about Paul. Rewind our journey back to Week One, Day Four. Read Acts 15:36–16:3 and refresh your memory concerning the circumstances that may have prompted Paul to make room in his ministry for an adolescent Timothy. What happened in Acts 15:37-39?

Paul would not take Mark on mission w/ him because Mark had failed him in the Past

Thank God desertion is not always final and failure isn't always fatal. Mark is proof. Quitter Boy made a comeback. Quitter Girl can, too.

Glance back at Philemon 24 and record what Paul called Mark and the three others: *his fellow workers*

Now read Colossians 4:10-11, written by Paul during an earlier imprisonment. Savor the layers of meaning in this literal rendering of the Greek regarding Aristarchus: "my fellow-prisoner of war."[13] List everything pertaining to Mark in these two verses of Colossians. *Mark's*

Cousin of Barnabas -
Coworker
Comfort to Paul

Thank God desertion is not always final and failure isn't always fatal.

Paul's request to the church in Colossae concerning Barnabas moves me each time I read it. What did he tell them to do (v.10)?

Welcome Mark if he showsup

Paul was not perfect. In his human nature, he was surely as capable of holding a grudge as we are. He could have interpreted their embrace of Barnabas as an act of disloyalty.

He didn't because division is anti-gospel. (Gospel math is multiplication.)

He didn't because rivalries are works of the flesh (Gal. 5:19-20).

He didn't because to do so would have dishonored Jesus and harmed the church.

He didn't because blackballing a servant of Jesus is dangerous hubris (Rom. 14:4).

We're advancing in our maturity when we resist equating our loved ones' acceptance of someone who hurt us as a rejection of us.

To make a comeback, people often need someone to welcome them back, *to invite* them back, but not necessarily to the same position or prior relationship. We welcome people back to their dignity in the body of Christ because Christ welcomed the recovering coward and quitter we saw in our mirrors this morning. Tribalism was as alive in first century Christianity as it is today. That the apostles resisted fostering team loyalty is refreshingly conveyed in the freedom of Silas and Mark to co-labor with both Peter and Paul.

> **READ 1 PETER 5:12-14.** (Silvanus and Silas are forms of the same name.) What did Peter consider Mark? *a son*

Helping set people up for a comeback doesn't cancel out warning people in harm's way of an unrepentant individual doing tremendous damage. Such was Alexander the coppersmith (2 Tim. 4:14-15).

> Glance back at 2 Timothy 4:12. Where had Paul sent Tychicus?

Ephesus

He probably sent him ahead to fill Timothy's spot so the young pastor could quickly depart. If Timothy left right away, he "could arrive at Rome in three or four months."[14] Tychicus was among Paul's coworkers on his third missionary journey. An interesting part of his bio is that "he had likely carried the Letters of Colossians (Col 4:7-9) and Ephesians (Eph 6:21)"[15] from Paul's hands to the recipients. Since the Greek verb tense translated "I have sent" in 2 Timothy 4:12 could also translate "I am sending," it's possible Tychicus carried this letter as well.[16]

Spot Troas again on your map. Why did Paul want Timothy to go through Troas on his way to Rome?

To get Pauls cloak, parchments + scrolls

Had some sudden arrest in Troas forced Paul to leave behind his possessions? We can only wonder. But his deep desire for those belongings in his final days is touchingly clear. The cloak was a heavy sleeveless outer garment much like a poncho. Paul's request, in view of his urgency for Timothy to come before winter (v. 21), suggests he longed for the cloak to help keep him warm in the cold. His humanness here is moving. It also sweeps aside the assumption that staunch servants of God don't shiver when they're cold. Paul's apostleship did not immunize him against the purple bruising of his shackles. It did not fill his empty stomach. It did not lull him into a baby's sleep on that brutal floor. (Compare 2 Cor. 6:4-5.)

> *Timothy was also to bring Paul's "scrolls." The Greek is biblia, from which comes "Bible." Biblion meant "a paper, letter, written document"… But its common use in the NT, as in the literature of that day, is for a "roll" or "scroll." These were probably made of papyrus.*
>
> *Paul especially wanted his "parchments." This kind of writing material was more expensive than papyrus; membrana (a Latin word, only here in the NT) were scrolls or codices written on animal skins (vellum). These may have been leather scrolls of OT books.[17]*

We can't say for certain Paul requested Scripture but neither can we easily imagine he wouldn't. After all, we probably would. We'd take any Bible in our time of desperation but we'd most want our own. The one smudged by our fingertips and tears. The one worn at the edges by our woes. The one we'd held to our chests in our crises. The one we'd turned from cover to cover in our searching, hoping, and studying. *Somebody bring me my Bible.*

We're not trapped in dungeons but some of us may be in hospital rooms, treatment facilities, or jail cells. And we can all imagine ourselves confined in some way.

If captive, what three personal possessions would you desire most?

Something to play music ~~or~~ on
Paper + pen
Bible

Paul had one visible thing in that damp prison cell as pen fell to paper in his final letter. Verse 11: _Luke_
is with me.

He had a friend. Luke stands as an anomaly in our day of celebrity. He was the kind who'd give up the right to a spotlight to live in somebody else's shadow. A highly educated Gentile doctor, believed to be from Antioch, tore roots from home and practice to attend to a small bald man with a hooked nose and crooked legs. The Greek who'd write the Gospel of Luke and Acts, pops into Paul's company for the first time in Acts 16:10 when the pronoun switches from "they" to "we."

Luke may have suddenly joined the apostle for medical reasons. Just prior to the doctor's arrival on the scene, Paul had been in Galatia (Acts 16:6). His words to the Galatians add the intrigue: "you know that previously I preached the gospel to you because of a physical illness" (Gal. 4:13). Had he and Luke become friends earlier when Paul served in Antioch? Had Luke then been summoned to come to the apostle's aid after his illness in Galatia? Whatever the circumstances, God was at the helm steering all things for gospel-good.

Any normalcy Luke might have enjoyed in Antioch he likely never possessed again. However, normalcy may be the fair price to pay for a one-way ticket to a divine adventure. At times Paul and Luke served separately, but countless miles bore the prints of both sets of feet. Luke was on the third floor in Troas when Paul preached so long that a young man named Eutychus fell asleep, then fell out the window to his death. Perhaps the doctor tried to reach him but Paul had Eutychus covered, holding him tightly, assuring the crowd he'd be okay. And he was (Acts 20:5-15).

Luke was also there with Paul and a boatload of other prisoners on a ship tossed like toothpicks by a northeaster on the Adriatic. He was there when they threw the ship's gear overboard. He was there when they got no glimpse of sun or stars and abandoned hope of being saved. He was there for 14 days when they were lost at sea and couldn't eat. He was there when Paul announced an angel of the Lord had appeared to him and assured him their lives would be spared. He was there when the ship ran aground and broke to pieces and they swam on planks to Malta's shore. He was there when a viper darted from a campfire and fastened onto Paul's hand. He was there when Paul shook it off and suffered no harm.

And he was there in that filthy dungeon in Paul's last days. Luke not only heard the great apostle dictate his final letter. He likely was the one who recorded it. Perhaps the physician's head was down as he listened carefully.

Crescens has gone to Galatia. Luke dipped the quill and inscribed it.

Titus to Dalmatia. Luke dipped the quill and again inscribed.

Only Luke is with me.

Q&A

Terri: *How do you combat worry when it comes to your children?*

Beth: *Whew. Is anything more challenging? I wish I always handled worry obediently but I don't. When I do, however, it's often the same way: confessing my trust in God and commanding my soul to be at rest in Him. I try to catch myself mid-worry and replace my anxious thoughts with prayer and, if possible, out loud and coupled with thanksgiving. "Thank You, Lord, for how much You love _____ and for the good You want to do her and for the plans You have for her…" I also ask Him often to deliver them from evil.*

Did the weathered apostle's voice crack when he dictated those five words? Did Luke pause when he heard them? Did he keep his head down or did he look up from the scroll and meet the eyes of his fellow wayfarer? Did tears roll clean streams down the silted face of the death-row inmate? Or did the two men simply smile and nod?

Luke, "the dearly loved physician" (Col. 4:14). To look the dying in the face, to face their fears right by their side, to enter their extreme discomfort to comfort, to offer companionship in their terminal loneliness: These things are sacred. These are not obligations of the Hippocratic Oath. These are the salve of saints.

Things on My Mind, Part 2

III. ENDURE HARDSHIP (2 TIM. 4:5)

"Endure hardship" (4:5) is, without a doubt, my favorite phrase from 2 Timothy. When we are enduring hardship, we tend to wonder what we've done wrong and if God is disciplining us. Maybe sometimes that is the case. But Paul makes space for precisely the opposite scenario. He says that anyone who wishes to live a godly life will, in fact, be persecuted (3:12). Persecution counts as hardship, don't you think?

So, if everyone around you is thriving and you are being as faithful as you can be but can't get a break:
Trust in God.
Resist bitterness.
Take your share.
Endure hardship.
Strengthen yourself in grace.

Paul is not eight verses into this letter before he invites Timothy to suffer with him for the gospel. Actually, he says it twice: "Join with me in suffering ..." (1:8; 2:3). What an invitation, right? I hope he used beautiful gold calligraphy for those lines. Paul meant the words he said. He was writing from a prison cell, and a number of his friends and associates had deserted him (4:10,16).

When we Christians romanticize suffering, I get uncomfortable fast. It is one thing to talk about suffering and quite another to actually endure it. I've experienced enough suffering in my own life to be sobered by it so supremely that I nearly don't have language for it. But I've also experienced far less suffering than the majority of people around the globe. This brings me a great deal of anxiety and pause when I try to form words about suffering. There is this profound section in Marilynne Robinson's novel Gilead where the elderly pastor Reverend John Ames says something that enters my mind often:

> "I heard a man say once that Christians worship sorrow. That is by no means true. But we do believe there is a sacred mystery in it, it's fair to say that ... This does not mean that it is ever right to cause suffering or to seek it out when it can be avoided, and serves no good, practical purpose. To value suffering in itself can be dangerous and strange, so I want to be clear about this. It means simply that God takes the side of sufferers against those who afflict them."[5]

The tension here is evident, yet we Christians are still left to try and answer Alan E. Lewis' profoundly important question: "What does it mean to be Christian, to be the church, God's people, if even the people's God renounces majesty and safety, risking pain, humility, and death, as the only way to secure on earth the coming reign of justice, grace, and peace?"[6]

We are left to make sense of what the cross of Christ might mean for us, what it means to pick up our own cross and follow in the steps of Jesus, like Paul and Timothy did (1:11-12).

In Parker Palmer's book *The Promise of Paradox*, he says, "The way of the cross is often misunderstood as masochistic, especially in an age so desperately in search of pleasure. But the suffering of which Jesus spoke is not the suffering that unwell people create for themselves."[7] Palmer says in an interview with *On Being*:

> "It's awfully important to distinguish in life, I think, between true crosses and false crosses. And I know in my growing up as a Christian, I didn't get much help with that. A cross was a cross was a cross, and if you were suffering, it was supposed to be somehow good. But I think that there are false forms of suffering that get imposed upon us, sometimes from without, from injustice and external cruelty, and sometimes from within, that really need to be resisted ... I believe that the God who gave me life wants me to live life fully and well. Now, is that going to take me to places where I suffer, because I am standing for something or I am committed to something or I am passionate about something that gets resisted and rejected by the society? Absolutely. But anyone who's ever suffered that way knows that it's a life-giving way to suffer, ... And that knowledge carries you through. But there's another kind of suffering that is simply and purely death. It's death in life, and that is a darkness to be worked through to find the life on the other side."[8]

I think Parker Palmer is right about the importance of distinguishing between true and false crosses. These are matters to be discerned with people in the faith whom we love and most of all by the power of the Spirit as we each continue to be faithful in the individual ways God has called us. As the old Rev. Ames said, we Christians don't value suffering in itself.

In the end, even the cross is not the end.

"The way of the cross reminds us that despair and disillusionment are not dead ends but signs of impending resurrection."[9]

Well. I can't believe we're here, but impending resurrection seems like a great place to conclude. If you know me at all in real life, you know I'm the absolute worst with good-byes, so this is me skipping that whole sad and awkward part and fumbling around anxiously. Some books, even biblical ones, they have you from the start. But 2 Timothy slowly took me by surprise. I didn't intend to fall for it, but I did. I'm grateful to God for the humbling grace of spending a portion of my life reading this rich text with you. Thank you for reading my words.

"The saying is trustworthy and deserving of full acceptance, that Christ Jesus came into the world to save sinners, of whom I am the foremost. But I received mercy for this reason, that in me, as the foremost, Jesus Christ might display his perfect patience as an example to those who were to believe in him for eternal life. To the King of the ages, immortal, invisible, the only God, be honor and glory forever and ever. Amen" (1 Tim. 1:15-17, ESV).

Day Five

BUT THE LORD

FLASH FORWARD: *But the Lord stood with me and strengthened me, so that the proclamation might be fully made through me and all the Gentiles might hear.*
2 TIMOTHY 4:17

Hebrews 1:3 says Jesus sustains "all things by His powerful word." Twenty-two brutal and beautiful years have blown off the calendar since my first Bible study hit the shelf. Through Christ's unfathomable grace, the wonder that someone actually sits on the other side of this page studying the Bible with me has never evaporated. God alone knows why I have had the privilege to serve you but I'm deeply grateful.

I received news earlier from my daughter that Jackson, her firstborn, had just gotten his final 4th grade report card. All A's. He set the goal last fall and labored hard toward it. Each six-week cycle he'd get so close. We told him incessantly how great he was doing but the boy had a goal. This was the last report card of the year and he did it. We cheered and fist-pumped our shoulders nearly out of joint. Other classes and challenges lie ahead but today we celebrated. You, my friend, will also have other classes and other teachers. Calmer ones I hope. But this teacher wants you to know you've made all A's and that she's cheering for you all the way from these Texas woods. You can add a "+" to that "A" if you want. One remaining assignment awaits you in the epilogue following this lesson. I hope you'll complete it. It will mean so much to someone.

Our journey's official ending is the Session Six video. Even if you haven't been able to view the previous sessions, please try to view the last one so we can have a proper wrap up and sending forth.

FOR NOW, LET'S READ PAUL'S FINAL WORDS IN 2 TIMOTHY 4:16-22. If you've handwritten the segments throughout the study, may God drench you with satisfaction as you write the conclusion.

Which one of these seven concluding verses stands out to you most and why?

17 - God gave me strength to get the message to the Gentiles

The verses are packed with such meaning, landing on one may be difficult. Did you catch the mystery in verse 20? An apostle who'd performed miracles was forced to leave a beloved co-laborer ill in Miletus. Unbelief wasn't the problem. Paul had "kept the faith." The problem was a fallen world, a system broken by sin, subjecting humanity to frailty and death. Wonders are glorious and exceptional graces performed, not by the whim of exceptional people, but by God alone. Many of us have witnessed miracles and also wept for lack of one. In those baffling moments when we know God can and wonder why He won't, we turn to 2 Timothy 4:20 and find peculiar comfort: "I left Trophimus sick at Miletus." Every missing miracle creates a cavern we can leave wide open to bitterness or decide to fill with faith. Trust holds a torch in the blackest hole. There the miracle is you. It's me. The great wonder is that the darkness did not overcome us.

> Blessed are those who have not seen and yet have believed.
> JOHN 20:29, ESV

Have you ever desperately wanted a miracle but God made you the miracle instead? If so, please share how.

Bob + Me coming to Christ

Reflect on 2 Timothy 4:16-17. Paul could and sometimes did take desertion personally. Why do you think his perspective varied here?

not sure

Paul's "first defense" probably refers to "a preliminary investigation ... called in Latin legal language the *prima actio*. This would have a purpose similar to a grand jury hearing."[18] Whether it ultimately led to his current imprisonment or referenced one earlier is unclear. Every detail fades into the distance and every player flees center stage when the One and Only makes His presence known.

But the Lord stood with me. Take pause. Don't move past this phrase quickly because this is the divine x factor. The grudge robber. The blame killer. When Jesus comes through in a remarkable way, we end up glad everyone else was out of the way. This, like nothing else, is what prompts us from the depths of our ransomed hearts to let others off the hook. We don't have to be deserted to feel all alone. All it takes is being in a place no one else can fully enter. They would if they could but they lack what it takes. Then, just when you think the isolation will overtake you, there He is. You can't see Him with your eyes. You can't hear Him with your ears. But the Spirit of Christ within you bears such witness to the presence of Christ beside you that you know you're not in it alone. When everyone else is everywhere else, He is there. Sometimes He chooses in His mercy and sovereignty to make you extraordinarily aware that He is.

Trust holds a torch in the blackest hole.

When everyone else is everywhere else, He is there.

Recall a time when you experienced the Lord in this way. Share your story.

Work was crazy computers down, customers yelling at me, employees literally 7-8 at a time yelling updates I prayed "Help pleae" + (Calm)

I vividly recall sitting on the hearth one morning while it was still pitch black outside feeling beaten up emotionally and worn down spiritually. I'd come under vicious attack the day before and had hardly slept all night. I rested my head in my hands and slumped my shoulders, considering how much easier life could be for my family and me if I had a less public ministry. I'd been happy all those years ago in that small Sunday School room with a handful of women to teach. I longed in that moment to go back and lock myself in that room with them. After a few miserable minutes of feeling sorry for myself, I began to whisper the words, "Worthy is the Lamb." I said them over and over and, with each repetition, my voice grew a little stronger. Then my weary body followed suit. I lifted my head off my hands and sat up straight and said the words again. "Worthy is the Lamb." Then I stood to my feet and proclaimed them with robust volume. Soon I paced across the floor of my den, full of faith and confidence in Jesus, praising Him with everything in me. The sense of His presence was so thick in that den for those few moments that I wanted to hold onto it forever. The change it brought in me was swift and dramatic. It could only have been Jesus.

> Scripture is our concrete in a world of mud.

For five weeks we've pounded on the absolute priority of sound doctrine. We must hold tightly to the Word of God, rightly dividing it and accurately teaching it. Scripture is our concrete in a world of mud. The church without the Bible has no floor. The Jesus-follower without the Bible has no feet. We stand on the authority of the Word of God or we won't stand at all. We must not add to it. We cannot subtract from it. Nothing overrules it. No prophetic word compares to it.

In the pages of Scripture we find a God who can be experienced. Not every claimed experience is genuine nor is any sensory experience necessary for a close walk with Jesus. We walk by faith, not by sight, and by knowing, not feeling. Anything contrary to the Word of God we summarily dismiss. But if we dismiss every possible way that Christ might choose to make His presence, comfort, affection, or direction known in a particularly perceptible way *unopposed to Scripture,* we could miss grace intended to get us through.

> *"But the Lord stood with me and _____ me, so that ..."*

"Enedunamōsen me" translates "Poured power into me"[19] and "infused me with strength ... made me dynamic!"[20] What was true for Paul is often true for other followers of Christ. When Jesus ordains or permits circumstances that bring us to a place of Population 2, He intends to strengthen us *so that* a vital part

of our calling can be fulfilled. If He wants us hyper-focused on Him alone, He wants to supply us with something we get from Him alone.

> Go back to the italicized sentence and underline "But the Lord." Now circle the phrases "stood with me" and "strengthened me." Lastly underline "so that."

Jesus is never unkind or haphazard. He is always at work *so that*. We may not see what lies on the other side of those two words until we're all the way home but we walk on by faith. Our future is pregnant with purpose. Your enemy the devil wants to trivialize and taunt you with "so what?" just so he can hijack "so that." Don't let him.

Paul had a future even on death row. He'd been crucified with Christ for 30 years. He was about to be more alive than he'd ever been in his life.

> *We have no ancient record of the trial; but Tertullian, writing about 200, reports that Paul was beheaded at Rome; and Origen, about 220, writes that 'Paul suffered martyrdom in Rome under Nero.' The emperor who condemned him died a coward's death, and soon nothing survived of his inordinate works. But from the defeated Paul came the theological structure of Christianity, as from Paul and Peter the astonishing organization of the Church.[21]*

Nero could take Paul's head but he could not take Paul's future. That day by the edge of a blade on the Via Ostia just outside of Rome, the body of Paul of Tarsus dropped to the ground. A body scarred up, bruised up, torn up, used up. Let the earth make dust of it. Paul had somewhere else to go. And, when he arrived, the One who'd spoken to him and through him, who'd stood with him and by him, stood right in front of him.

We don't know for certain if Timothy made it in time but this we know: Jesus did. We're not sure if Paul ever got his cloak or if he shivered through winter. If his shoulders stayed bare, surely Jesus held him in His arms even if the old apostle couldn't feel it. We also can't be sure if Paul ever got his scrolls and parchments. If he didn't, he had words that God etched upon his heart from the time he was knee-high to his daddy and reciting the *Shema* for the very first time.

> Paul closed the tender letter with a two-sentence benediction. Write 2 Timothy 4:22.

> Circle the word "your" in the first sentence. This pronoun is singular and intended for Timothy. Label his name above it.

Some of us want more from Paul as he directs his last personal word to the young pastor. After all, Paul had no one else like Timothy (Phil. 2:20). If we were concluding a letter to someone we cherished, we'd want to tell him we loved him. But, you see, Paul didn't wait until the end. He said it from the beginning.

To whom is the letter addressed in 2 Timothy 1:2?

Return to your handwritten version of 2 Timothy 4:22. Draw a rectangle around the word "you" at the end of the second sentence. This final word is a plural pronoun: Grace be with *you all*. Here in this gorgeous simplicity we know Paul anticipated that his letter to Timothy was not only *for* Timothy. Paul foresaw the Ephesian believers on the other side of the scroll. The Holy Spirit, unencumbered by time, also saw us.

> For now we see indistinctly, as in a mirror, but then face to face. Now I know in part, but then I will know fully, as I am fully known.
>
> 1 CORINTHIANS 13:12

The prolific pen of the apostle Paul spilled its last drop. Timothy would indeed fulfill his calling and courageously fight the good fight until he, too, was martyred. The letter has since fallen into the hands of generations of believers for though its inspired author was chained like a criminal, "God's word is not chained" (2 Tim. 2:9, NIV).

We haven't spent weeks in Bible study to add to a stack of workbooks. God wooed us here and used Paul's final letter to strengthen us *so that* ...

_____

I can't fill in your blank. You can't fill in mine. Only Jesus can fill them. But we can fulfill them. With all that we have and all that we are, let's do.

O _____, guard the deposit entrusted to you.
Fulfill your ministry.
Hold on to the pattern of sound teaching ... in the faith
and love that are in Christ Jesus. Guard, through the Holy
Spirit who lives in us, that good thing entrusted to you.

You have the globe. You have the gospel. You have the gifting.

Go, mighty servant.

Group Session Six

WATCH THE VIDEO—FACE TO FACE

INTRODUCTION

No writer of the New Testament canon was inspired to more forthrightly encourage us and stir up our anticipation about our future lives than the apostle Paul. As his earthly life draws to a close in his second letter to Timothy, we will read and reflect on some of those iconic encouragements.

1. Paul had an _unapologetic_ _expectancy_ of _reward_ .

2. Paul anticipated _direct_ _interaction_ with _Christ_ .

3. Paul anticipated an _Exceedingly_ _vivacious_ _Existance_ in a _Kingdom_ .

4. Paul never equated " _heavenly_ " with _translucent_ .

5. To _see_ _that_ _face_ would be to _fully_ _know_
   as _he'd_ _been_ _known_ .

6. Paul knew what we _must_ _know_ _to_
   ~~thrive~~ : not _one_ _ounce_ of our _labor_
   will _~~least~~ ever_ _be_ _in_ _vain_ .

Handwrite 2 Timothy

2 Timothy 1

entrusted

2 Timothy 2

entrusted

2 Timothy 4

entrusted

Epilogue Assignment

We've learned so many things over our five-week journey, but, foundational to them all, we've embraced the value of a personal letter. By God's gracious design, Jesus-followers through the centuries have gotten to literally read Timothy's mail and, if willing, to be postmarked by it. The most appropriate way possible to fold up his letter and tuck it back in the envelope of our New Testaments is by composing one of our own to someone we hold dear in the faith. This will be our final way to honor the paradigm that has become significant to us as well as the individuals it represents in our own lives.

Do you have an individual in your life, outside your immediate family, you get to parent or mentor to some degree in the faith? You may be too new to Christianity to have poured into others so don't feel pressured to say yes. On the other hand, some of you in high school or college have already had enough discipleship to take others under your wing. Of whom would you say at this moment in your life (as Paul said of Timothy) I have no one else like him/her? If you can't make up your mind between two, go ahead and list them both. Paul considered both Timothy and Titus to be sons in the faith.

_____   _____

Do they know how you feel about them? How you thank God for them? Pray for them? What confidence you have in their divine gifting? Do they know how much you consider Jesus worthy of pouring out every drop of lifeblood to serve? Have you ever encouraged them in writing to be fearless and faithful? Would you consider writing him/her/them as we narrow our journey to a close? Imagine what a treasure your letter would be in a day when abbreviations and emojis are common means of communicating. Your letter doesn't need to be long. It just needs to come from someplace deep.

If you're too young in the faith to have a Timothy or two, turn the letter around and imagine it from Timothy to Paul instead. Consider writing someone who has been a Paul-figure to you. Express ways you've been profoundly affected and highlight specific things you've learned or gained from the individual. I've provided two pages, both front and back, for the composition of these personal letters. Use them as you wish. You are welcome to write either one long letter using all four pages or two letters that each fit within a single front and back. If you're blessed to be in that brief window of time when you have both a Paul-figure and Timothy-figure in your life, think of writing each of them. Carefully cut out the pages, write the letters then mail them or give them to the recipients. God alone knows what meaning and timing your words will have in their lives.

Dearest love to you, faithful follower of Christ Jesus. What joy you must be to Him to attend to every last line of a study. May God drench you in His astonishing favor, "he who is the blessed and only Sovereign, the King of kings and Lord of lords, who alone has immortality, who dwells in unapproachable light, whom no one has ever seen or can see. To him be honor and eternal dominion. Amen" (1Tim. 6:15b-16, ESV).

entrusted

entrusted

Endnotes

INTRODUCTION
1. Woodrow Wilson, as quoted in "How It Feels to Be President," *The Independent*, Vol. LXXVII, (New York, NY: The Independent Weekly, Inc.: 1914), 439

WEEK 1:
1. Strabo, *Geography* Translated by H.L. Jones (Cambridge, MA: Harvard University Press, 1932), 16.
2. W. A. Elwell, & B.J. Beitzel, *Baker Encyclopedia of the Bible* (Grand Rapids, MI: Baker Book House, 1988), 16.
3. C. W. Draper with Harrop Clayton, "Jewish Parties in the New Testament," *Holman Illustrated Bible Dictionary*, eds. C. Brand, C. Draper, A. England, S. Bond, E. R. Clendenen, & T. C. Butler (Nashville, TN: Holman Bible Publishers, 2003), 917.
4. Ibid.
5. Ibid.
6. "Sha'uwl," *Blue Letter Bible* (online), cited 11 July 2016. Available on the Internet: *blueletterbible.com*.
8. Timothy George, *Galatians, The New American Commentary*, Vol. 30 (Nashville, TN: Broadman & Holman Publishers, 1994), 77-78.
9. F.B. Meyer, *Paul: A Servant of Jesus Christ* (New York, NY: Fleming H. Revell Company, 1897), 23.
10. R.J. Dean, "Sanhedrin." *Holman Illustrated Bible Dictionary*, 1445.
11. Ibid.
12. N.T. Wright, *What Saint Paul Really Said* (Grand Rapids, MI: William B. Eerdmans Publishing Company, 1997), 25.
13. Talmud: Shabbat 31a.
14. N.T. Wright, *What Saint Paul Really Said*, 21
15. N.T. Wright's translation of the Greek in *Paul and the Faithfulness of God* (Minneapolis, MN: Fortress Press, 2013), 518.
16. *NET Bible First Edition* (Richardson, TX: Biblical Studies Press, LLC, 1996), Acts 16:1.
17. R. J. Dean, "Timothy" *Holman Illustrated Bible Dictionary*, 1597.
18. J.B. Polhill, *Acts, The New American Commentary*, Vol. 26, 343.
19. T.D. Lea & H. P. Griffin, *1, 2 Timothy, Titus, The New American Commentary*, Vol 34, footnote for Irenaeus, Against Heresies.
20. George W. Knight, III, *The Pastoral Epistles, New International Greek Testament Commentary* (Grand Rapids, MI: Wm. B. Eerdmans Publishing Co., 1992), 205
21. J.B. Polhill, 342–344.

WEEK 2:
1. John MacArthur, *MacArthur New Testament Commentary: 2 Timothy* (Chicago, IL: Moody Publishers, 1995), 51.
2. I. H. Marshall, *The Pastoral Epistles* (New York, NY: T&T Clark LTD, 1999), 703.
3. R. Earle, *2 Timothy, The Expositor's Bible Commentary: Ephesians through Philemon*, F. E. Gaebelein, ed., Vol. 11 (Grand Rapids, MI: Zondervan Publishing House, 1981), 395.

4. Spiros Zodhiates, S., *The Complete Word Study Dictionary: New Testament* (Chattanooga, TN: AMG Publishers: 2000), 1219.
5. Ibid.
6. Ibid., 1469.
7. Ibid., 1402.
8. William D. Mounce, *Pastoral Epistles, Word Biblical Commentary, Vol. 46* (Dallas, TX: Word Inc., 2000), 488.
9. Ibid.
10. Lea & Griffin, 197.
11. Zodhiates, 167.

WEEK 3
1. Lea & Griffin, , 204
2. Zodhiates, 576.
3. Mounce, 519.
4. Thomas C. Oden, *Interpretation: A Bible Commentary for Teaching and Preaching, First and Second Timothy and Titus*, (Louisville, KY: John Knox Press, 1989), 67-68.
5. Ibid., 68.
6. Ibid., 69.
7. Matthew Henry, *Matthew Henry's Commentary on the Whole Bible: Complete and Unabridged in One Volume* (Peabody, MA: Hendrickson Publishers, 1991), 2362.
8. Gordon D. Fee, *1 & 2 Timothy, Titus, Understanding the Bible Commentary Series* (Grand Rapids, MI: Baker Books, 1988), 258.
9. Lea & Griffin, 214
10. Zodhiates, 155.
11. W. E. Vine, M. F. Unger, & W. White, Jr., *Vine's Complete Expository Dictionary of Old and New Testament Words*, (Nashville, TN: Thomas Nelson, 1996).
12. Zodhiates, 703.

WEEK 4
1. "Eschatology," *Merriam-Webster*. Available on the Internet: *merriam-webster.com*
2. Earle, 406.
3. Knight, 429–430.
4. Ibid., 431.

WEEK 5
1. Mounce, 571.
2. Zodhiates, 939.
3. Robert W. Wall, *1&2 Timothy and Titus, The Two Horizons New Testament Commentary*, (Grand Rapids, MI: William B. Eerdmans Publishing Company, 2012), 276.
4. John Calvin, *The John Calvin Bible Commentaries: Harmony of the Law*, Vol. 2 (Grand Rapids, MI: Christian Classics Ethereal Library, 2009), Kindle edition.
5. Mounce, 574.
6. Lea & Griffin, 247.
7. Will Durant, *The Story of Civilization: Caesar and Christ* (New York, NY: Simon and Schuster, 1944), 572.
8. *The Annals and History of Tacitus: A New and Literal English Version* (London: Forgotten Books, 2015), 363.
9. Earle, 412.
10. Mounce, 579.
11. Ibid., 578.
12. Earle, 413.

13. P.T. O'Brien, *Colossians, Philemon, Word Biblical Commentary*, Vol. 44 (Dallas, TX: Word Inc., 1998), 249.
14. Lea & Griffin, 250-252.
15. Ibid., 253.
16. Earle, 414.
17. Ibid., 413-415.
18. Lea & Griffin, 255.
19. A. T. Robertson, *Word Pictures in the New Testament* (Nashville, TN: Broadman Press, 1993), 2 Ti 4:17.
20. Earle, 416.
21. Durant, 591.

NEXT LEVEL WITH MELISSA

WEEK 1
1. N.T. Wright, *Simply Christian* (New York, NY: Harper-Collins Publishers, 2006), 181.
2. Benjamin Myers, *Christ the Stranger: The Theology of Rowan Williams* (T & T Clark: New York, 2012), xi.
3. George Milligan, *The New Testament Documents: Their Origin and Early History* (The MacMillan Company: New York, 1913), 77.
4. Shauna Niequist, *Bread & Wine* (Grand Rapids: Zondervan, 2013), 258.

WEEK 2
1. Fred Sanders, "C. H. Dodd and Realized Eschatology," *The Scriptorium Daily* (online) 7 April 2009 [cited 11 July 2016]. Available on the Internet: *scriptoriumdaily.com*.
2. Ibid.
3. Michael Horton, *A Better Way: Rediscovering the Drama of God-Centered Worship* (Grand Rapids, BakerBooks, 2002), 126.
4. Ibid.
5. Ibid., 127.
6. Ibid., 130.
7. Ibid.
8. Ibid., 128.
9. Krista Tippett, *Becoming Wise*, (New York: Penguin Press, 2016), 148, emphasis mine.
10. Horton, 128.
11. Gordon D. Fee, The First Epistle to the Corinthians, NICNT, (Grand Rapids: Eerdmans, 1987), 174-175.
12. Ibid.

WEEK 3
1. *The Book of Common Prayer* (New York: Church Publishing Incorporated), 358-359.
2. *The Book of Common Prayer*, 358-359.
3. John Webster, "Confession and Confessions," in *Nicene Christianity: The Future for a New Ecumenism* (Grand Rapids: Brazos Press, 2001), 104-105.
4. Webster, 112
5. Stephen Holmes, "Creed," in *Dictionary of Theological Interpretation of the Bible* (Grand Rapids: Baker Academic, 2005), 146.
6. Ibid.
7. Ibid.

8. See a fuller list here: J.N.D. Kelly, *Early Christian Creeds*, 3rd Edition, (London and New York: Routledge, 2972) 13.
9. Ibid., 17.
10. R. P. Martin, "Creed," in *Dictionary of Paul and His Letters*, Gerald F. Hawthorne, Ralph P. Martin, Daniel G. Reid, Eds. (Downers Grove, IL: InterVarsity Press, 1993), 191.
11. J. L. Wu, "Liturgical Elements," in *Dictionary of Paul and His Letters*, 557.
12. N. T. Wright, *Paul for Everyone: The Pastoral Letters: 1 and 2 Timothy and Titus* (Louisville, KY: Westminster John Knox Press, 2004), 103-104.
13. Mark Yarbrough, *Paul's Utilization of Preformed Traditions in 1 Timothy: An Evaluation of the Apostle's Literary, Rhetorical, and Theological Tactics* (New York, NY: T & T Clark, 2009), 54.
14. R.P. Martin, 191.
15. E. E. Ellis, "Pastoral Letters," in *Dictionary of Paul and His Letters*, 665.
16. Yarbrough, 142.
17. Kelly, 19.
18. John Newton, "Amazing Grace."

WEEK 4
1. Francis Spufford, *Unapologetic: Why, Despite Everything, Christianity Can Still Make Surprising Emotional Sense* (New York: HarperOne, 2012), 196.
2. John Fleter Tipei, *The Laying On of Hands in the New Testament: Its Significance, Techniques, and Effects* (Lanham, MD: University Press of America, 2009), 1.
3. Robert F. O'Toole, "Hands, Laying on of" in *Anchor Bible Dictionary* Vol. III Ed. David Noel Freedman (New York: Doubleday), 48-49.
4. Tipei, 178.
5. Robert Wall and Richard B. Steele, *1 & 2 Timothy and Titus* (Grand Rapids: Wm. B. Eerdmans Publishing Co., 2012), 224.
6. F. F. Bruce, *The Pauline Circle* (Eugene, Oregon: Wipf & Stock Publishers, 1985), 30.

WEEK 5
1. Tippett, 29.
2. Ibid
3. David Kinnaman and Gabe Lyons, *Good Faith* (Grand Rapids, MI: Baker Books, 2016), 58.
4. I. Howard Marshall, *Dictionary for Theological Interpretation of the Bible* (Grand Rapids, MI: Baker Books, 2005), 805.
5. Marilynne Robinson, *Gilead* (New York, NY: Picador, 2004), 161.
6. Alan E. Lewis, *Between Cross and Resurrection: A Theology of Holy Saturday* (Grand Rapids, MI: Wm. B. Eerdmans Publishing Co., 2001), 101.
7. Parker Palmer, *The Promise of Paradox* (San Francisco, CA: Jossey-Bass, 1980), 32.
8. Parker Palmer, "Soul Depression," *On Being* podcast 26 February 2009. Available on the Internet: *onbeing.org*.
9. Palmer, *The Promise of Paradox*, 33.

191

LIVING PROOF *live*
with **Beth Moore**

The ultimate live Bible study event.
Experience Living Proof Live with your study group!

lifeway.com/livingproof

LifeWay Women | events